TYPE PLAYER 2

ISBN: 978-1-58423-433-3

First Published in the United States of America by Gingko Press
by arrangement with Sandu Publishing Co., Limited

Gingko Press, Inc.
1321 Fifth Street
Berkeley, CA 94710 USA
Tel: (510) 898 1195
Fax: (510) 898 1196
Email: books@gingkopress.com
www.gingkopress.com

Copyright © 2011 by SANDU PUBLISHING

Sponsored by: Design 360° – Concept and Design Magazine
Chief Editor: Wang Shaoqiang
Executive Editors: Daniela Huang, Winnie Feng
Chief Designer: Wang Shaoqiang
Book Designer: Antiny Wu
Sales Managers:
Niu Guanghui (China), Daniela Huang (International)
Address:
3rd Floor, West Tower,
No.10 Ligang Road, Haizhu District,
510280, Guangzhou, China
Tel: (86)-20-84344460
Fax: (86)-20-84344460
sandu.sales@gmail.com
www.design360.cn
www.sandu360.com

Cover project by Tim Fishlock

Printed and bound in China

Foreword Backward

By Ian Lynam

Type designers often find using their own type an alien concept. Over the weeks, months and years spent refining a body of type, their work often comes to feel precious. Often, type designers are reluctant to push the boundaries of what they can do with their own type. For example, look at most contemporary typeface specimens — they are designed to highlight the type, but not necessarily what can be done with the type. History, development, ligatures, alternate characters, and basic text settings are shown off, but nine times out of ten, the quest to show type as a tool outshines the specimen as a piece of good design. Case in point: during a recent outing to Los Angeles for TypeCon, the esteemed international typography conference, I was graced with a giant goody bag of type specimens, the bulk of which were decent specimens but not so outstanding that I was convinced to hire the designers for anything except text type. To me, this is a tragedy — the inability of the type industry at large to impart a sense of the exciting potential type design possesses.

I've designed lettering and fonts for years, but I feel as if I have just begun designing truly formal "type." I was playing with the design of type well before I became a "legitimate" designer. This has always been countered with a sensibility to utilize more masterful designs to complement my own informal experimentations. I could (almost) always sense when my goofy attempts didn't work or weren't refined enough for application, but I kept playing, trying, working away at both the refined and the jubilant. That being said, I still insist on using more formal designs within my own graphic design work for assorted media when the need arises. I tweak and fix spacing as I discover errors, add ligatures as needed, and add new weights when the need arises (and the user license allows). Designing new type and editing existing type within the context of a body of design work helps increase the relevance and utility of type designs.

A big part of this actively participatory perspective has been my digitization of Oswald Bruce Cooper's work over the past few years for my type foundry Wordshape. Cooper was the genius behind the typeface Cooper Black and a half-dozen or so other typefaces chock full of personality, moxie, and irreverence. Most of these typefaces have seen poorly drawn and spaced digital versions released to the public over the past few decades, as well as a number of designs left in the dust, forgotten and just waiting to be exhumed. Seeing the countless revisions Cooper put into his work — dozens of fully articulated drawings for the lowercase "m" of Cooper Black Italic alone — has imbued me with a newfound respect for the process of designing type. This is type design — creating variations on a theme and refining letters down to the purest version. In Cooper's time, this was done in context: he'd draw individual letterforms and also try them out by incorporating versions within advertisements for assorted clients before official public release. Cooper could gauge contextual use in advance showings that were hand-rendered and simultaneously promote his own design and typesetting firm.

It is this point of in-use refinement that offers those making type and lettering of a playful, experimental nature an advantage: the ability to have fun, test, and work out a type design before public release (if applicable). Alternately, a designer can make a one-off, shedding the preciousness of the refined, and in this way creating the theoretical and physical space appropriate to case-specific applications, in lieu of preconceived formulas culled from copying others' work.

This willingness to leap into the creative fray has caused me to develop a newfound respect for Cooper. His work, alongside his contemporary William Addison Dwiggins, is one of the "losers" of history — the goofy analog to the more "refined" work of the Bauhauslers and their search a generation later for a purified (though, in retrospect, just as goofy) universal form of type and lettering. The former members of the Bauhaus are the ones remembered best in the timeline of graphic design history. Cooper's types, however, see multifarious applications in contemporary society, whereas one is hard-pressed to find the type designs of Herbert Bayer in use today. True typographic innovation shines through the gauze of the historical veil, no matter how heroic a position one has been ascribed.

Who knows what role the history books will assign designers active today in expanding the boundaries of visual language, particularly those most stalwart in exploring the realms of intercultural communication. Satya Rajpurohit, Peter Bil'ak, and Rajesh Kejriwal of the Indian Type Foundry are contemporary type designers in pursuit of communicative efficacy — their foundry is currently developing unified digital versions of all the major scripts in India: Bengali, Devanagari, Gujarati, Gurmukhi, Kannada, Malayalam, Oriya, Tamil, and Telugu. These designers are pursuing a means of allowing unified communication within India and related areas utilizing a formalized body of work. These efforts offer up a concentrated foray into truly increasing communicability between cultures. Will they be remembered for these efforts? Elsewhere, we find ourselves at a specific moment in history — one fraught with an overabundance of humanist sans serif types designed to pursue a utopian sense of form in typeface design. We do not need another riff on the mechanized humanist Klavika theme nor the smooth humanist Frutiger/Myriad theme. We need to see an increase in exploring type design in cultural areas where we as a race are deficient.* Perhaps where we are most deficient is in the constant search for the ultimate neutral type, one that embodies pure communication without disclosing an era or hint to context. My response is this: Timelessness is a myth. Inflection is unavoidable and should be embraced. The market is already flooded with recurring variations on said theme. The past decade in graphic design has largely been a myopic look backward in time with aesthetics to match. My hope is that the bulk of graphic design from this decade will be seen as merely a blip of constipation, not an end point.

The mode of contemporary *style* for most citizens of the world is to be boring and reflexive. If contemporary design is a matter of styling/cultural hairdressing, then most stylists have relegated themselves to the corners of the design sphere where haircuts are offered with a maximum of efficiency and affordability. Stylists demoted to the position of service providers — and such style has a place — make average things average for an average world. But there are those who strive to overstep boundaries, to lead, and to fail harder and faster than their contemporaries in pushing style forward. There are those like myself who look to history in order to help inform the present, who look to the screw-ups from the annals and are continually fascinated with the awkward and the off. Therein lies the future — in doing it all wrong.

We need the weird and the truly experimental in order to push contemporary aesthetics. We need the playful. Without it, we are merely treading water, and while that may make us fit, it won't get us very far.

And we are deficient. Try designing a book in Vietnamese and see how many fonts are on offer.

Bio: Ian Lynam is a graphic designer and writer living in Tokyo. He runs a multidisciplinary design studio that focuses on pan-cultural identity design, motion graphics, and editorial design. He is a graduate of Portland State University (B.S. Graphic Design) and California Institute of the Arts (M.F.A. Graphic Design). His most recent book is *Parallel Strokes*, an inquiry into the crossroads of graffiti and type design. He writes regularly for "Idea Magazine," "Néojaponisme," and a host of design books.

CONTENTS

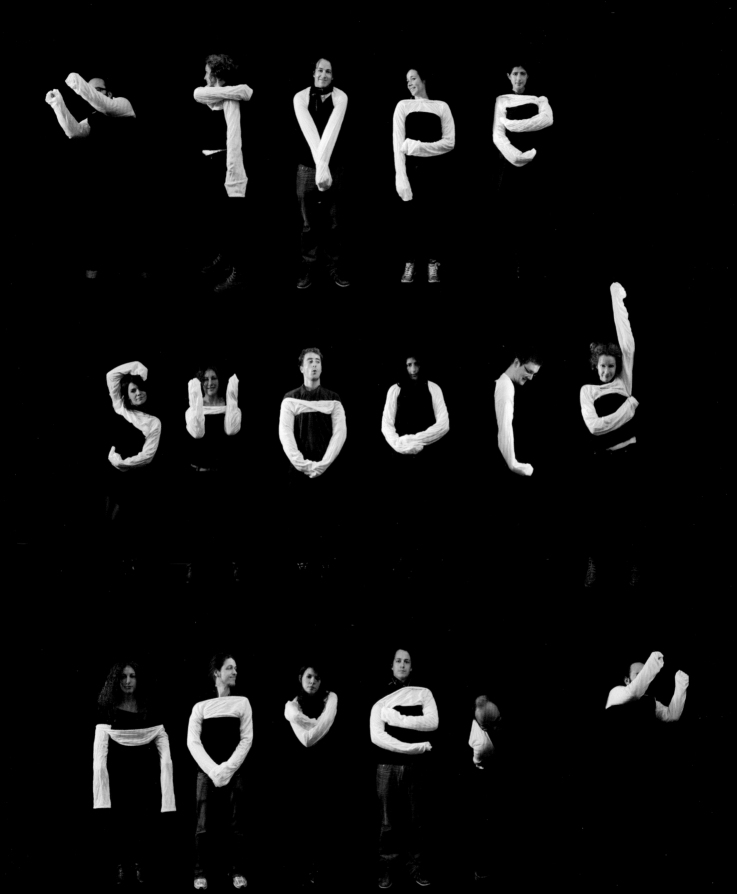

"The idea is to create a 'readable experience rather than a scripted space.' Building up three-dimensional typographic installations allows confrontation between words and real life, using context as a playground rather than a simple background."

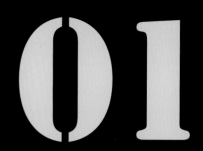

How did you get started designing type?

Typographic installations allowed me to integrate my two loves, photography and installation, and to focus on semiotics, and how to influence the meaning and impact of a message. I also see it as a chance to use mediums that are usually not related to graphic design.

More generally, I'm passionate about finding alternatives to print and computer-based communication; I love working out other solutions to publicly display physical messages in highly visible ways, taking their environment into account.

The idea is to create a "readable experience rather than a scripted space," (an idea borrowed from Michael Worthington). Building up three-dimensional typographic installations allows confrontation between words and real life, using context as a playground rather than a simple background.

What inspires you the most? Are there any type designers or movements that you find particularly inspiring?

Puns, Freudian slips, English and foreign idioms are an untarnishable source of inspiration. Playing with words and idea association in general. Georges Perec and OULIPO's work. I'm fascinated by little ways to both enhance and disrupt the everyday.

Andy Goldsworthy's ephemeral and natural print work (Rain Shadows), any in situ work by Helmut Smits and the Russian art group Voina are amongst my influences, and I've recently become fascinated by Chinese artist Chu Yun's work.

Your design work is described as focusing on the "temporary" and "transient nature of things." Take the example of "Letterform for the Ephemeral." How do you apply this concept to typography? Can you share your favorite moment during the design process?

In *The Practice of Everyday Life*, Michel de Certeau creates a relationship between the metropolis and its inhabitants on one side, and the practice of writing and speaking on the other side, and discusses how pedestrians are "writing an urban text as they move through it."

A given message evolves in perpetual flux and its context is constantly shifting, regardless of whether its is an advertisement or public signage. Who is its audience? Where is it read? What is the weather like? What is everyone talking about on that day? Are they in a hurry? Does it smell of hot dogs as people are reading it? A static printed message cannot adapt to a changing

situation; it therefore belongs to the platonic ideal world rather than the hic et nunc (here and now) of the real world.

Because of the instability of the circumstances of message delivery, a context is bound to change and never be the same twice, just like Heraclites' river.

This thought leads me to concentrate my research on referencing the passing of time.

The wearable letterform allows comment on situations as they happen: a group of people standing in a public place can spell out a comment by becoming different letters, one word at a time, a bit like an analogical tweet (from Twitter) that would involve a group of people rather than an expression of individuality.

What is left of that kind of performance is a trace of it, as the message displayed (at the time the photograph was taken) will not be accurate anymore when looking at the photograph. What was achieved with this experiment of Wearable Type is a hic et nunc letterform, a letterform for the here and now, finding its raison d'être when used in real time.

I think that my favorite moment during the design process is when I get to the hands-on stage of the work, literally making things exist. There is something magical about making readable a pile of books, a few objects, or a group of people.

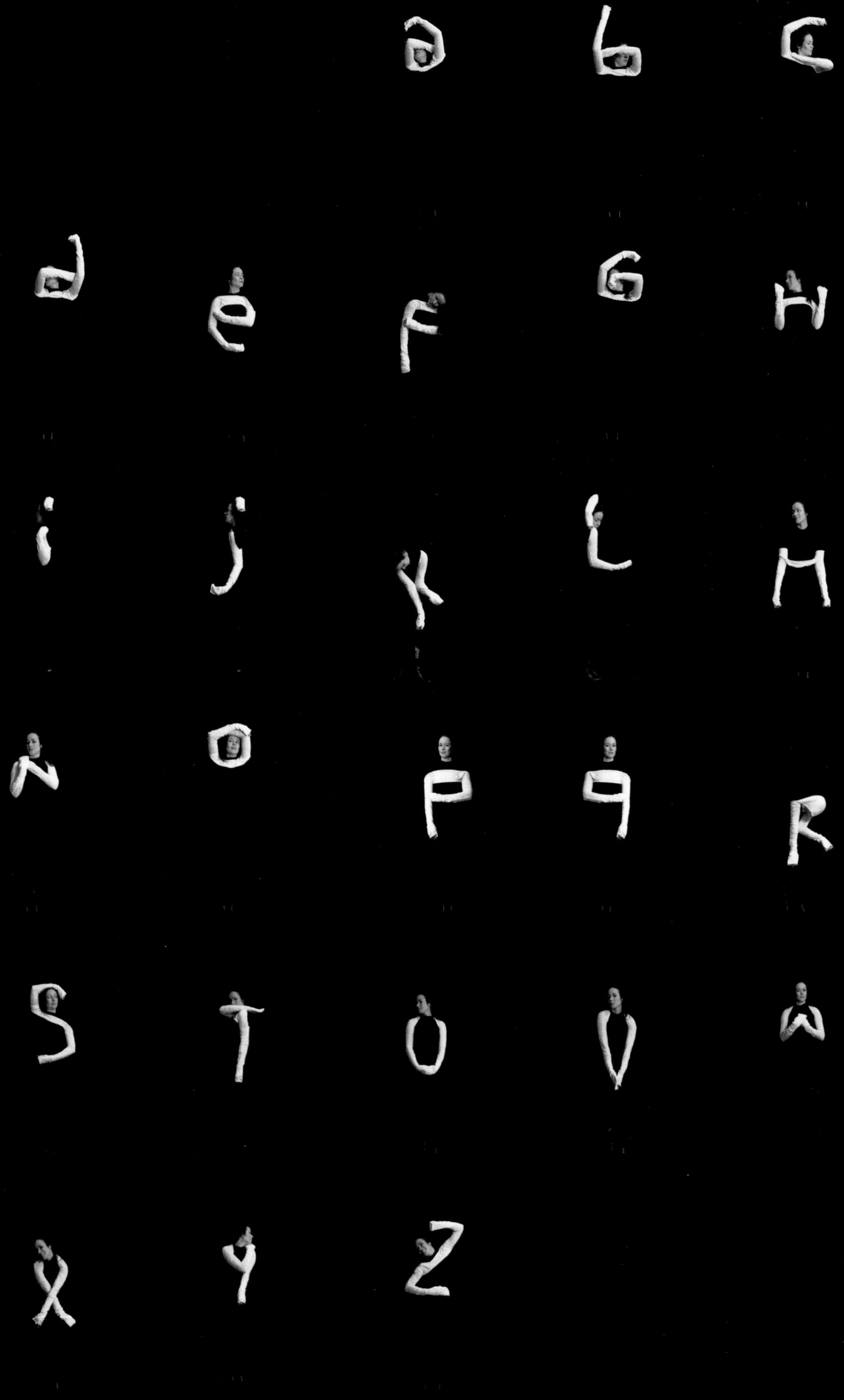

"I thought, 'I can present typography in my own way, as I believe it is one of the territories that can accomplish a visual expression that functions as a communication tool as well as expressing the beauty of the form itself.' "

Interview with
NAM

How did you get started designing type?

I had been so interested in typography for a long time and wanted to take on the challenge of designing it. I started to design my own typeface because I thought that it is one of the territories that can accomplish a visual expression that functions as a communication tool as well as expressing the beauty of the form itself.

What inspires you the most? Are there any type designers or movements that you find particularly inspiring?

In this work in particular, I think the flag signals which I learned during my time as a Boy Scout gave me a first glance into type design.

I cannot acknowledge all of the designers I like because there are so many, but I think the philosophical typography by Mr. Stefan Sagmeister is magnificent.

"Kids Alphabet" is an interesting project that composes the alphabet out of real objects and surreal images. How did you integrate alphabet design with the physical world of children? Please share any challenges you encountered during the photo shoot.

I wanted this project to work as a visual piece as well as a typeface. I intended to imbue the photos with a mischievous feeling, so we planned the photo shoot as a play date for the children. The photo shoot was a little challenging as the models were kids and they didn't move in the ways we wanted them to. However, the flip side of their unpredictable movement was that they created wonderful forms we hadn't imagined — which made the photo shoot fun.

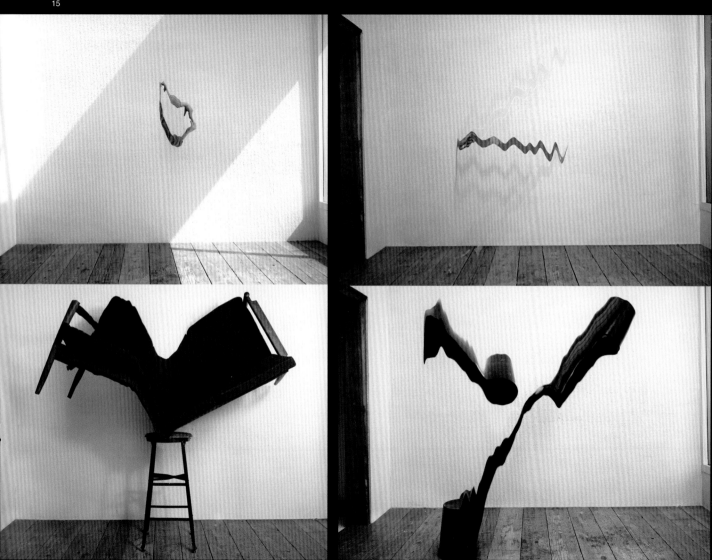

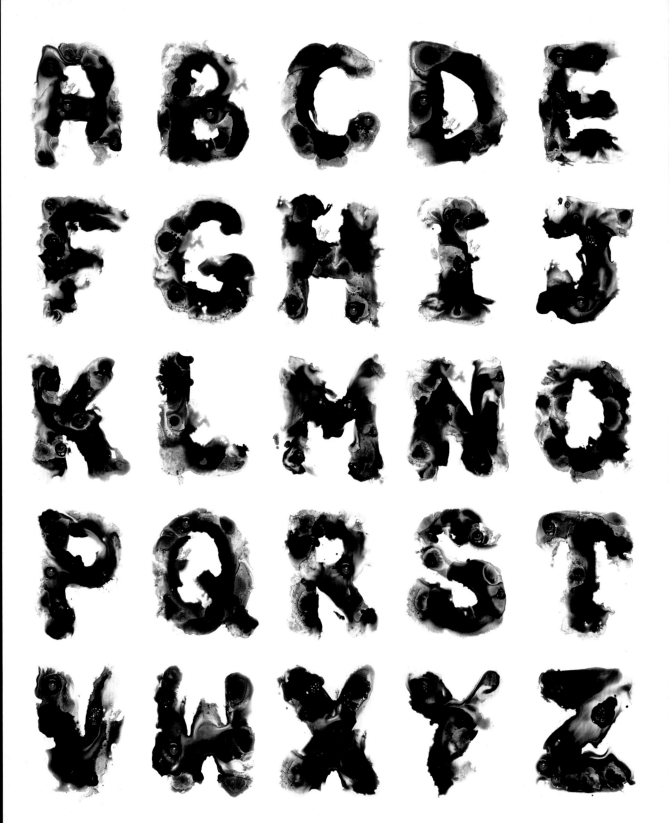

"Graphic design benefits our society — it is one of the most powerful tools today. It can shape people's minds and help make our world a much better and more interesting place in which to live."

How did you get started designing type?

I have always had an interest in letterforms, words, books and language. My obsession with typography started in design school, when I began photographing signs, words and letters that I came across in everyday life. I realized that typography is such a hugely powerful tool and means of expression.

During my last year at design school I designed my first typeface for an identity project. I had a desire to create a unique, bespoke typographical solution for the project. I started with a couple of letters I had created for the logo, and then developed this further by creating the entire alphabet. There was something really wonderful in seeing an alphabet slowly come together, letter by letter.

I managed to get a job a few months later at a small design studio, where I was lucky enough to be given design projects through which I could continue my typographic work.

What inspires you the most? Are there any typography designers or movements that you find particularly inspiring?

Most things inspire me. I find that inspiration can come from anywhere. I love to read. I love books, music, art, traveling and seeing this amazing world that we live in. I'm inspired by the people I meet, random things I find and objects I collect along the way. I often analyse the world, observe nature, explore, listen and always question everything; because everything in life is interesting if you look closely enough.

A creative and comfortable workspace is also very important for me. A place with fun, excitement and an inspiring atmosphere. If you truly care about the work that you create, you have to care about the space where it is created.

Another motivational factor is the belief that graphic design benefits our society. It is one of the most powerful tools today. It can shape people's minds and help make our world a much better and more interesting place to live in.

There are many great designers who have been a constant source of inspiration throughout my career. The spirited and witty work of Alan Fletcher, the beautiful designs of Herb Lubalin and Milton Glaser, the intelligent solutions of Dieter Rams, the incredible structure found in the work of Josef Muller-Brockmann. The list is endless.

Tiana, your works look very "playful, fun and experimental." Do you think you are able to place the least emphasis on function during the design process, since most of your projects are self-initiated?

Well, actually, I try to keep a healthy balance between client and self-initiated projects. I think designers need to find a balance between the need to earn money and doing work that inspires them.

I have always found that one of the most effective methods of inspiring your own creativity is through self-initiated projects. It can help a designer discover her personal tastes and individual passions.

Self-initiated projects are often opportunities to explore new techniques, step out of the design industry's influence, and take bigger risks. At the end of every self-initiated project, I've always emerged with new information and unique tools and processes to apply to my next studio project.

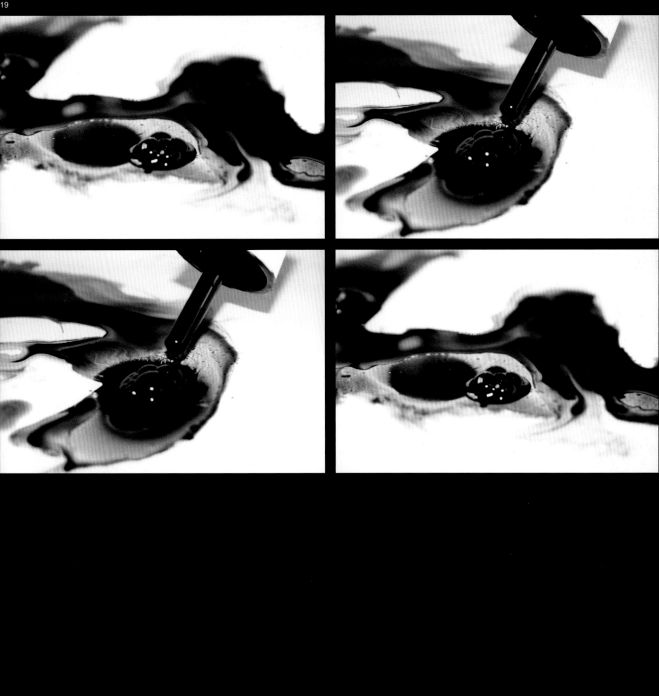

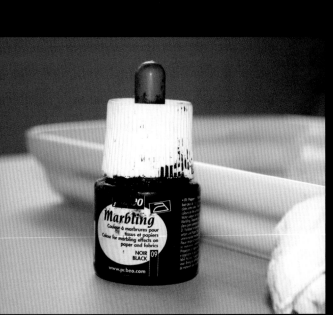

Design/ Roger Gaillard

ÂMES DAMNÉES

Type is an entity. Each letter is unique but arranged together, letters create a unified character. Each letter has its own identity which it communicates within the alphabet. Together, words and sentences are communicated through shapes. I see these typographic shapes like ghosts dancing — which can be represented by the plastic bag forms. I created these figures as I would a typeface — concerned with the negative and positive space, the shadows, the totality of the character, and the unity of the character. I thought about the shapes as a system, which for me is the definition of a typeface. I created this type project to learn and discover, which is the goal of every experience for me.

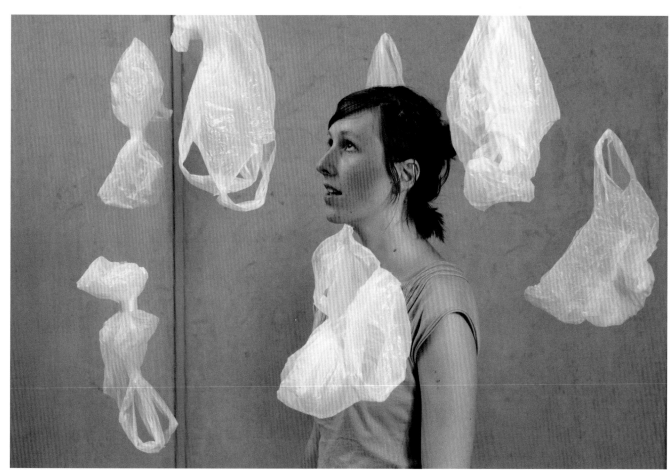

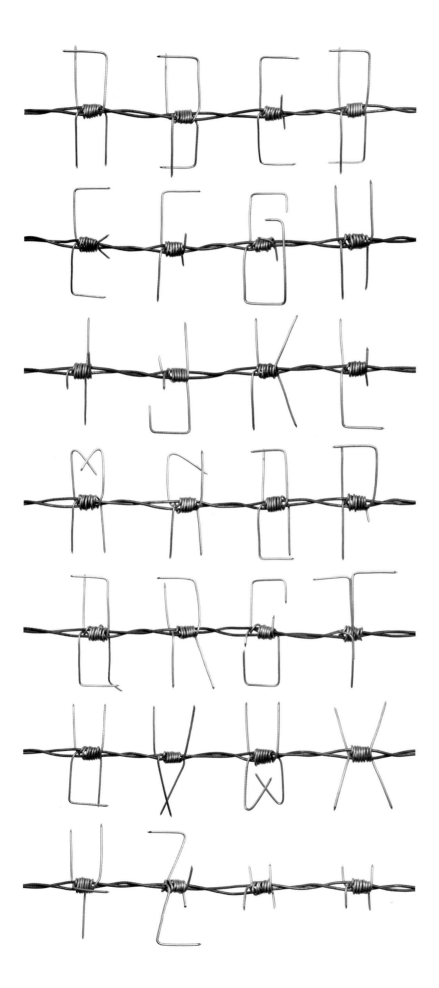

Design/ Andrew Effendy

THE DEVIL'S ROPE

I came up with this idea after seeing so many barbed wire fences in Skid Row, Los Angeles. After its invention, barbed wire was extensively used to create space divisions by agriculture, economic parties, political bodies, and the military. The concept was to form an alphabet by using the four barbs of the twisted wires. The same gauge steel wire and the exact spacing measurement between the barbs were maintained to create the same feeling as that inspired by real barbed wire. A mix of Vinegar and salt water was used to rust the metal wires by applying the mixture liberally to them for about a week. It is interesting to see how the barbed wire alphabet has such a strong visual impact and how people have different interpretations. The Native Americans called barbed wire "the devil's rope" because it caused hardships as a result of its use and because it hindered their nomadic lifestyle.

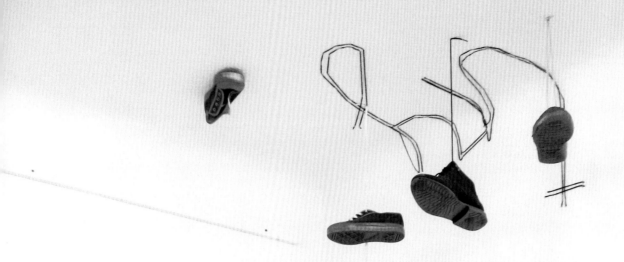

PLAY

"Play" was my final graduation project for the Academy of Fine Arts Maastricht in the Netherlands.

Working with real things in a three-dimensional space allows me to minimize the actual distance between myself and the object. This happens without any computer support. In my opinion, design feels more realistic and alive this way; it can be slightly inaccurate, but in a good way. This adds a sense of ease to my work. Handmade things show imperfections; this happens accidentally or as a result of experimentation. It is simply the side effect of having fun and playing around. Through hand-produced projects, the designer becomes involved with the image and becomes a vivid part of it. I believe design is all about fun. Play is the beginning of every invention, and it's how we learn. Play helps children learn to be adults by exploring the world, and it's how we feel alive. It's so easy — just play!

Design/ Akatre

LA GALERIE DES GALERIES
SPACE FOR FANTASY

Visual of the exposition and in situ installation.

Design Agency/ Zwölf
Design/ Stefan Guzy, Björn Wiede
Client/ SSC Group GmbH

THE SPARROW AND THE CROW TOUR

On "The Sparrow And The Crow" (Grönland), his second album to be released in Europe, US singer-songwriter William Fitzsimmons handles the theme of his recent divorce. We took the idea of a fight between sparrow and crow (in which they would both be sure to lose a few feathers) literally, and created a typographic photogram out of numerous sparrow and crow feathers.

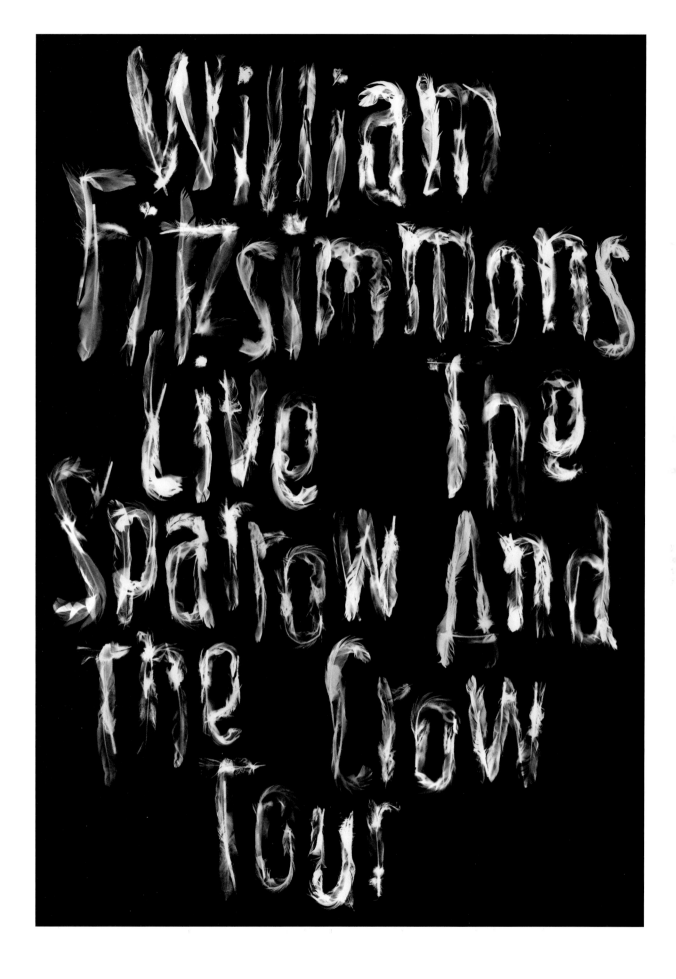

Design/ Ebon Heath

TYPOGRAPHIC MOBILES

Typographic Mobiles is a synthesis of our typographic language with the physical expression of our body language. These kinetic structures make the viewer "listen" with his eyes. The project is an exploration of how we can make sound and the linguistic symbols of sound be "heard" visually. We are intending to unlock the sleeping meaning latent in an authors' arrangement of letters and words — allowing it to be as free and expressive as its content. When words come alive, it will not be quiet. Words may yell or whisper, but they are all saying something.

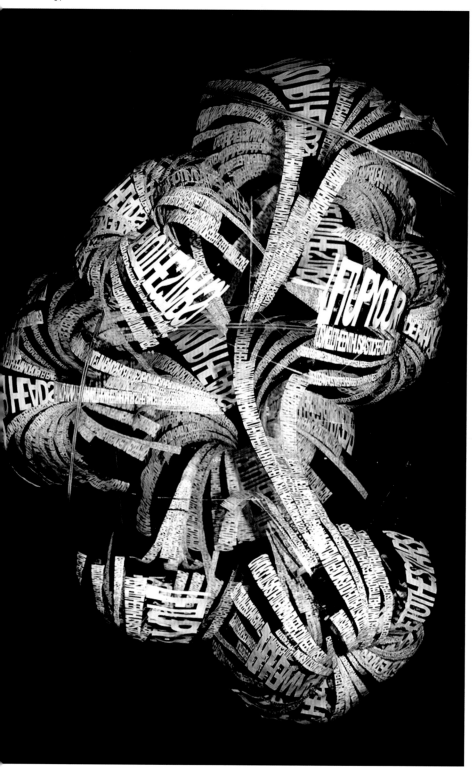

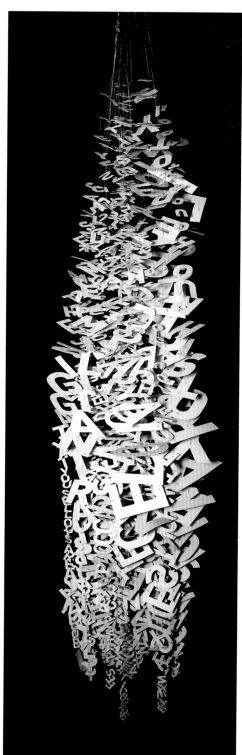

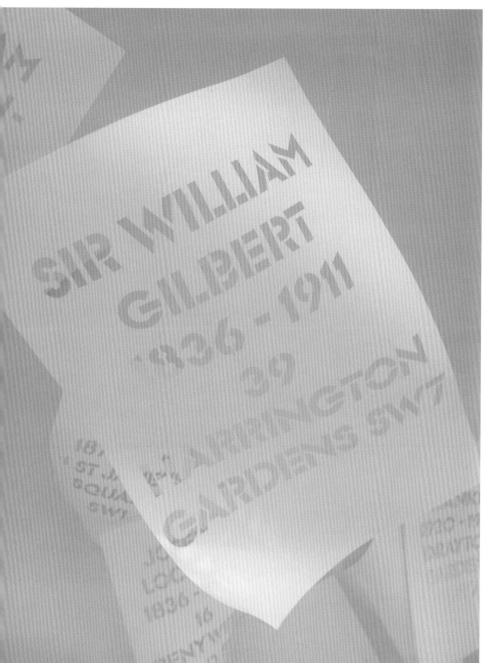

Design/ Shaz Madani
Client/ Douglas and Gordon
Commission/ Ideas Factory

DOUGLAS AND GORDON

Window installation for estate agents Douglas and Gordon in South Kensington. The result is a piece celebrating the famous residents of the borough of Kensington and Chelsea who have left their mark on the area and contributed to its rich history. The details of almost 200 plaques were laser cut into large sheets of paper, which were suspended from the ceilings and arranged within the windows of D&G.

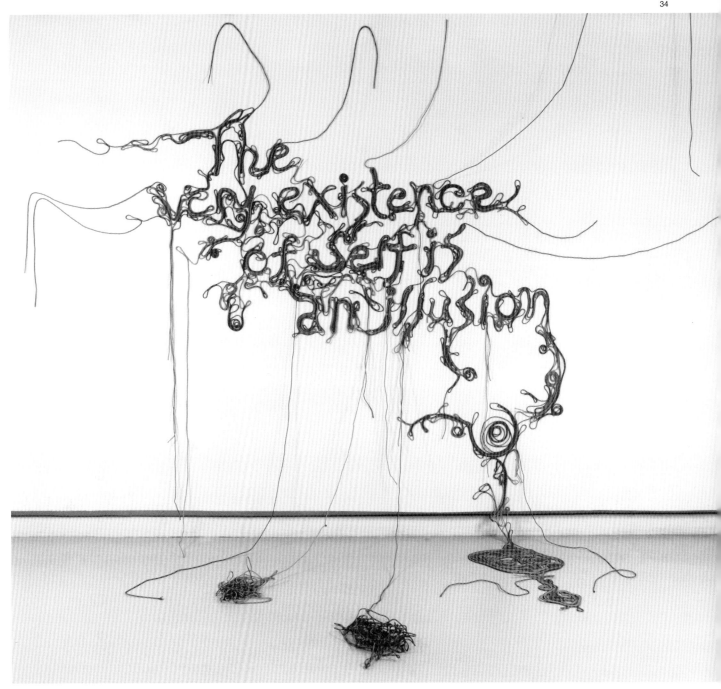

Design/ Elle Jeong Eun Kim
Client/ Self Initiated Work

EGO = ILLUSION

People grab on to an elusory notion of self
and all the desires, ideas and activities that will
feed that false construction. There can be no
peace and contentment unless we let go of
all the vanity of the self. This piece is a formal
exploration of expressive type, created with
repetitive loops of electric pink and orange
rope. The undulating linear quality of the
typographic installation challenges legibility,
reflecting the content of the text.

Design/ Farina Kuklinski

PLAY

"Play" was my final graduation project for the Academy of Fine Arts Maastricht in the Netherlands.

Working with real things in a three-dimensional space allows me to minimize the actual distance between myself and the object. This happens without any computer support. In my opinion, design feels more realistic and alive this way; it can be slightly inaccurate, but in a good way. This adds a sense of ease to my work. Handmade things show imperfections; this happens accidentally or as a result of experimentation. It is simply the side effect of having fun and playing around. Through hand-produced projects, the designer becomes involved with the image and becomes a vivid part of it. I believe design is all about fun. Play is the beginning of every invention, and it's how we learn. Play helps children learn to be adults by exploring the world, and it's how we feel alive. It's so easy — just play!

Design/ Madoka Takuma
Photography/ Nobu Yamaguchi

THE EVERYDAY USE OF ABC PACKAGING

Eco-packaging is increasingly becoming the only acceptable form of packaging today and reducing excess packaging has become a moral crusade for retailers. As a result, products are experiencing a "stripping down" of their outer casing. However, there remains a vital connection between the product packaging and product. The packaging delivers the emotion and the content delivers its function. As a product you cannot separate the two. This self-initiated project explores the intersection between package design and graphic design. The typographical theme acts as a sequential structure within which random everyday objects can seamlessly relate to one another and therefore find their place amid a jumble of objects. Each design has been taken from existing typefaces.

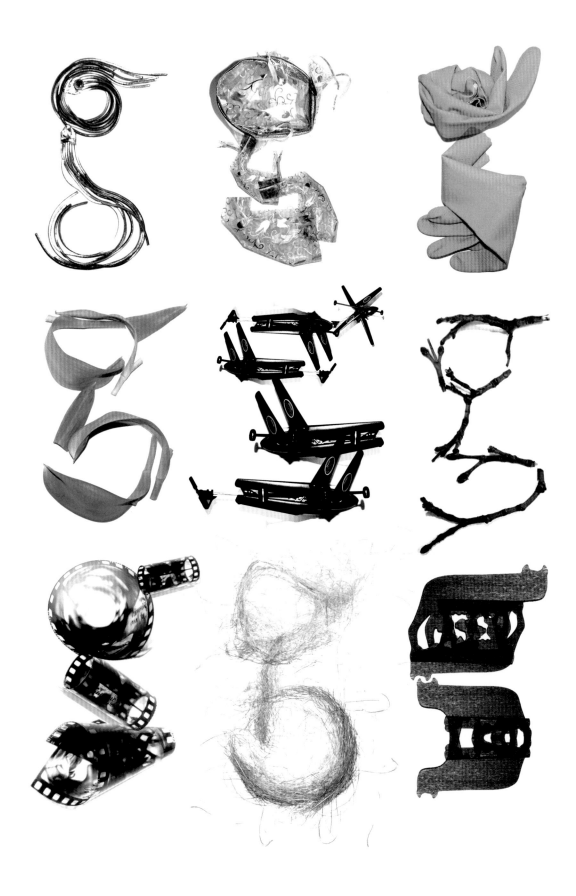

Design/ Sveta Sebyakina

MY FAVORITE LETTER G

Sveta's favorite interpretations of the letter G.

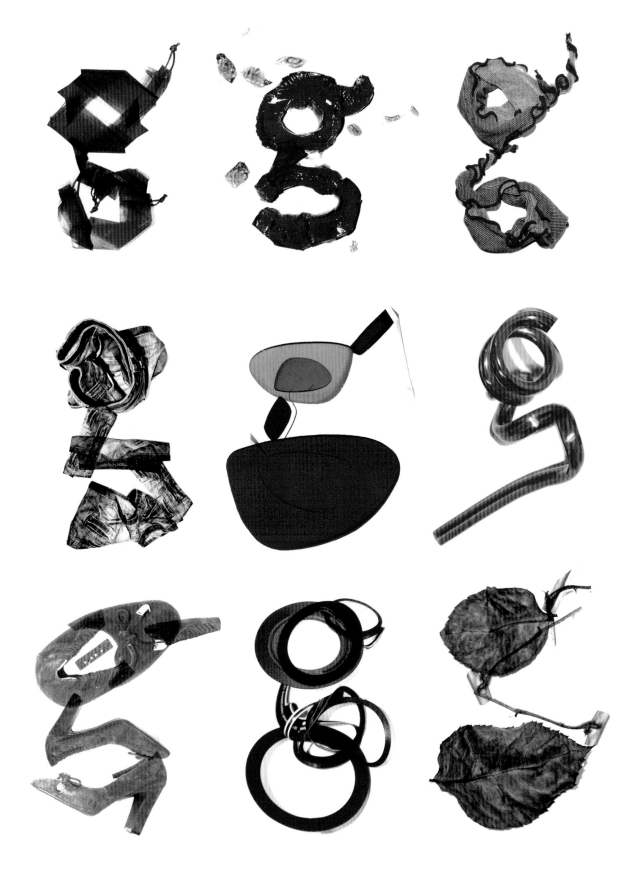

Design/ Jarrik Muller

3D TYPEFACE

This is a 3D typeface constructed out of paper. By cutting, folding and gluing the paper together you can create this 3D typeface.

Design/ Amandine Alessandra

BOOKSETTING

This series is based on Thomas Fuller's statement "A book that is shut is but a block." Shelves are used as a typographic grid; books are considered for their shape and color, rather than content.

Building up the letters reminded me very much of typesetting, as every type made of colored books had to be blocked with white books, just as it is done in letterpress, where large areas of white space are created by the wooden blocks called furniture.

Design Agency/ Snask
Design/ Snask + Dancemade
Client/ Malmö Festival
Photography/ Axel Engström, Lundholm

MALMÖ FESTIVAL

Malmö festival is the largest city festival in Scandinavia. With 1.5 million visitors each year, it is a hugely popular event held during 8 days in August. We worked with the festival coordinators from 2009 to 2010. We reinterpreted their identity to focus more on art and design, while keeping it playful and for the public. These installations focus on identity, concept and tone of voice in areas such as graphic design, magazines, ads, films, and the environment.

Design/ Stefan Sagmeister
Manufacture/ Bali Rattan (Indonesia)
Photography/ Karim Charlebois-Zariffa

THE TALKATIVE CHAIR

The text of this chair simply refers to a diary entry written while sitting on our balcony in Bali where the chair itself was ultimately placed. The designer very much loves sitting here looking out over the Sayan Ridge with a large pot of coffee and a medium size cigar and letting his mind go. Life is still good. Just saw a spectacular sunrise and now the incredible lush greens of the rice paddies pop his eyes out. His big toe appears to be very dirty. But it's just a bit of congealed blood underneath his skin, acquired during a morning walk through the jungle with John. The small mosquitoes are a pain, so tiny they are basically invisible. Their bites itch for days even without scratching. Stop sitting here staring into the air. Better get going! Take a shower and start the day proper; there certainly is enough to do here. He already has a whole list ready to go.

Design/ Elle Jeong Eun Kim
Client/ Self Initiated Work

UNTITLED

These two engraved wood posters are created with Elle's custom designed typeface called Echo and Smoke. Echo and Smoke is a typeface that requires the viewer to engage with the negative space to read the text. The typeface has two different variations: one with the vertical lines and the other without. These characters, which challenge legibility when arranged into sentences, are used to communicate self-reflective and diary-like texts.

Design/ Elle Jeong Eun Kim
Client/ Self Initiated Work

PHANTOM FUTURE

Elle is interested in the friction between our conscious and unconscious self, in other words between the Ego self and the Shadow self. Your shadow is the primitive side of your personality. This project started as an experiment. Elle had 14 people (including herself) imprint their movements while sleeping on a sheet of paper. When you fall asleep, your unconscious takes over, which leads to having dreams. Elle sees these imprinted papers as a record of our unconscious minds.

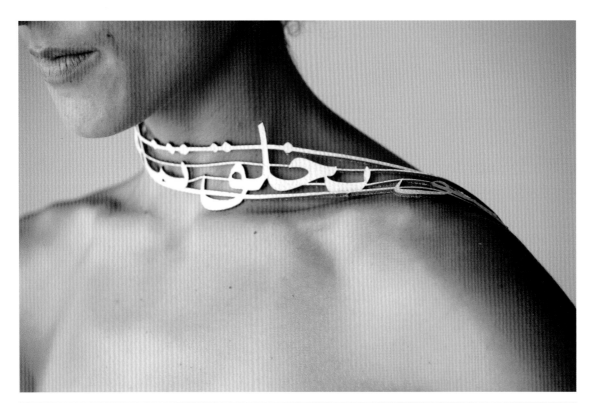

Design/ Ebon Heath

TYPOGRAPHIC JEWELRY

If we adorn ourselves with positive mantras, how does it inspire us to remember what we value and hold dear? This body art uses the same visual language as Ebon Heath's sculptural work, yet on a small enough scale to adorn an ear, arm, or neck. Different structures have been developed in laser cut leathers and acrylics. The first collection debuted in Dubai in 2009 and experimented with English and Arabic letter forms. Limited edition custom pieces are being commissioned, and currently the next collection is being developed in Balii to be available in fall 2011.

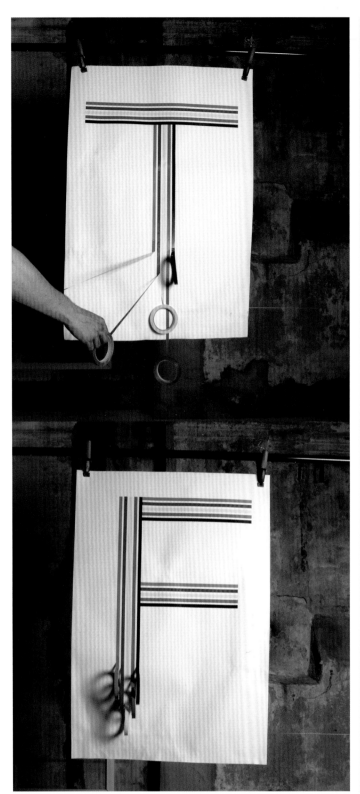
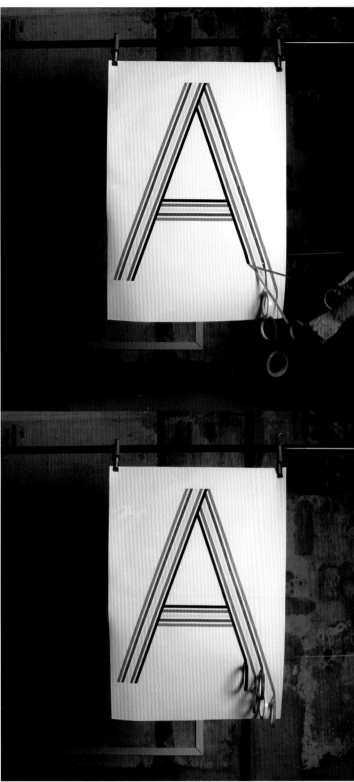

Design/ LoSiento

TAPE FACE

Typography made out of 5 different colors of adhesive
tape (masking tape). The name for the project comes
from combining MASKING TAPE and FACE and
adding to the ending of TYPE FACE. TYPE FACE is thus
reinvented as TAPE FACE.

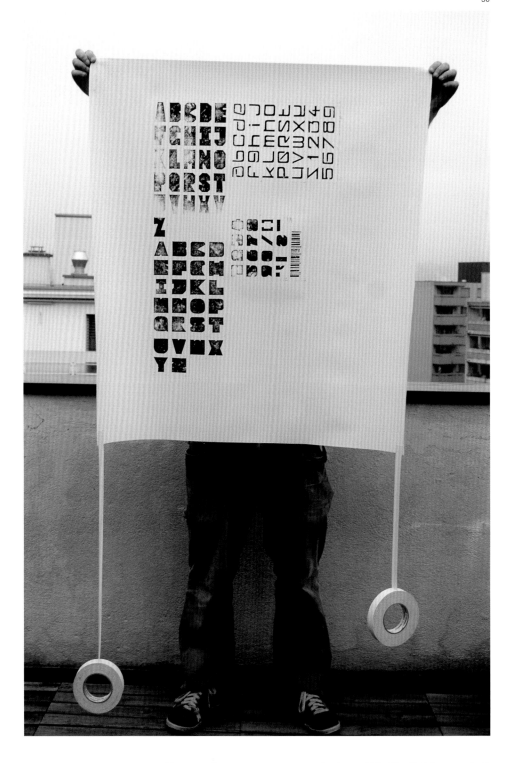

Design Agency/ Type Fabric | Atelier für Gestaltung
Design/ Type Fabric © and Fabio Parizzi
Client/ Self Initiated Work

F O N T – LYNOL TYPE DESIGN

For this project, we went back to the roots of type design by working by hand instead of using a computer or any other modern technique. We wanted to feel the physicality of carving, printing with simple techniques, and letting imperfections show their own type of beauty.

Design/ Nina Jua Klein

WE ARE ALL IN THIS TOGETHER

"We are all in this together" is a re-contextualization of the typeface developed for the project "Jekyll & Hyde" and was exhibited during the latter stages of the global financial downturn.

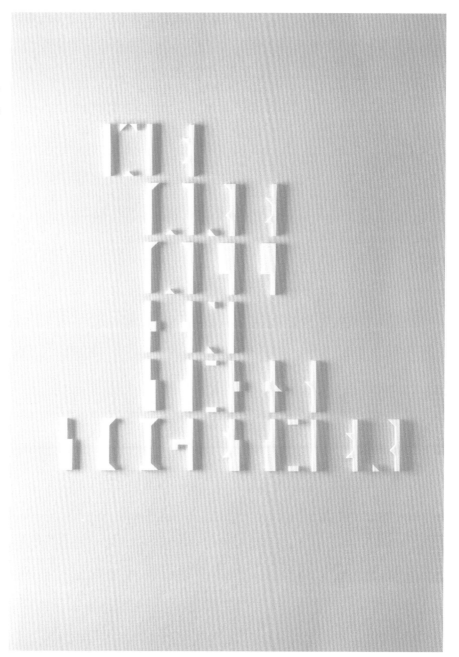

EMPO

EMPO is a psycho-osteopathy school and office. The project takes the study of the human body and its parts as a starting point. LoSiento decided to represent the organs and bone structure in a physical and volumetric form, using colored cardboard to go along with their search for a certain feeling of nostalgia for school.

At the same time, LoSiento started studying the way to create an exclusive alphabet for the project: it should "lift" in random volumes to hold an organic reminiscence. This randomness was then reconstructed through mathematics (using Pythagoras' theorem) to develop each character at a horizontal level, as well as to achieve a certain harmony within the whole typographic family. The material used for the alphabet is also cardboard, in a bone-like broken white color.

Design/ Sasha Prood

FIELD STUDY INSPIRED POSTER & CARD

Sasha Prood's goal of transforming vintage field illustrations into unique letterforms became a detailed study of nature — and another example of her true aesthetic. As a starting point for both of these works, she researched plant and fungi types to inspire an authentic visual variety. As she began drawing the letters, she carefully analyzed which plant or fungi would fit each letter in an effortless, organic way. As in her previous works, in this project she was striving for a natural — not molded — form of illustration.

Design Agency/ Ethanissweet
Design/ Ethan Park
Illustration/ Ethan Park
Copywriter/ Louise Sheperd
Client/ Self Initiated Work
Photography/ Ethan Park

VISUAL PROPOSAL : HOW TO TOUCH SOMEONE WITH POSTERS

The project was a visual proposal series for a promotional campaign at Kingston University. Leaves were collected and then manipulated to compose visual messages.

Design/ Jas Bhachu
Client/ Self Initiated Work

FONT GENERATOR

The project was the creation of a typographic font generator in order to produce a visual representation of the word "Move."

Using a Rubik's Cube, I designed a set of stamps to be placed on four sides of the cube so that users are able to create their own font.

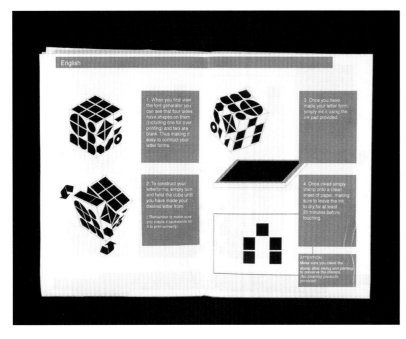

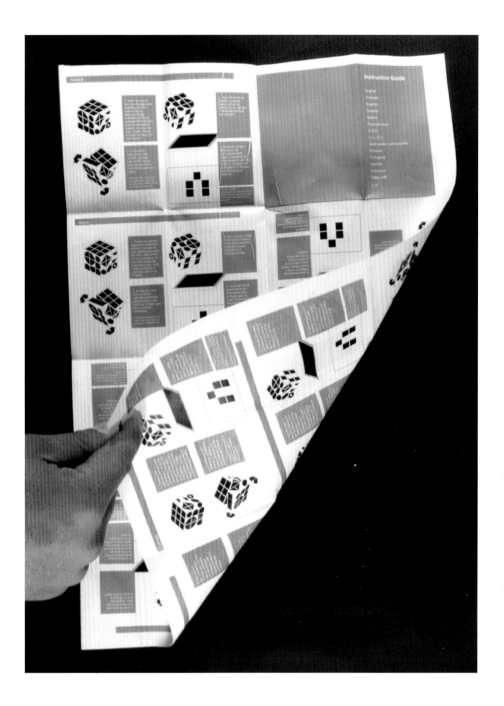

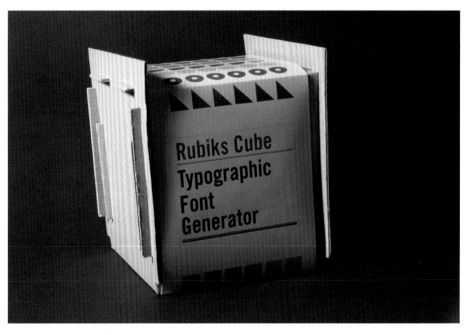

Art Direction/ De Designpolitie
Design/ Corriette Schoenaerts
Client/ Hogeschool voor de Kunsten Utrecht - HKU
(Art Academy Utrecht)
Photography/ Corriette Schoenaerts

QUOTES

These pictures were part of a marketing campaign for the Utrecht School of the Arts. Quotations by world famous personalities painted on big cardboard cubes reflect the ambitions of both the school itself and its (future) students. At the same time, these pictures try to represent the diversity of the school building.

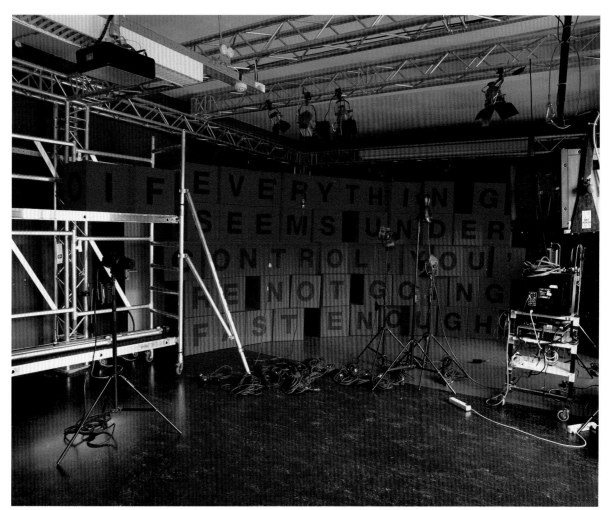

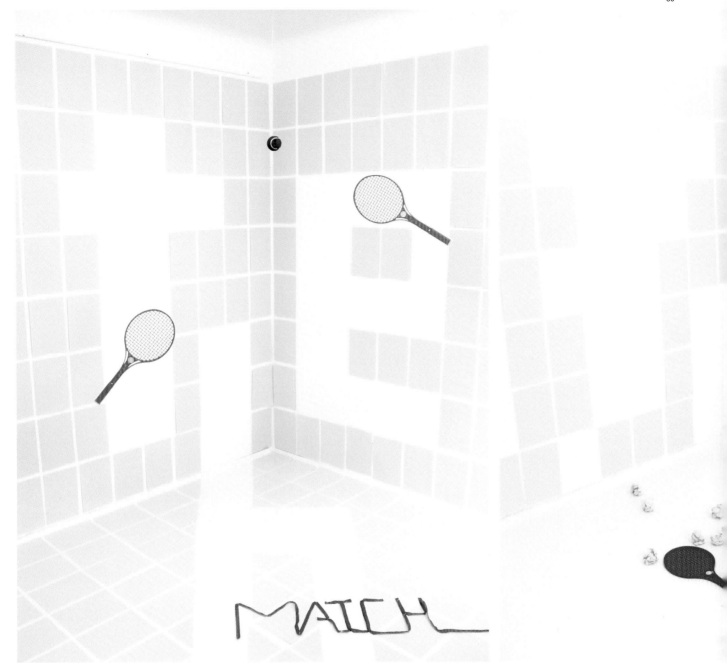

Design/ Farina Kuklinski

PLAY

"Play" was my final graduation project for the Academy of Fine Arts Maastricht in the Netherlands.

Working with real things in a three-dimensional space allows me to minimize the actual distance between myself and the object. This happens without any computer support. In my opinion, design feels more realistic and alive this way; it can be slightly inaccurate, but in a good way. This adds a sense of ease to my work. Handmade things show imperfections; this happens accidentally or as a result of experimentation. It is simply the side effect of having fun and playing around. Through hand-produced projects, the designer becomes involved with the image and becomes a vivid part of it. I believe design is all about fun. Play is the beginning of every invention, and it's how we learn. Play helps children learn to be adults by exploring the world, and it's how we feel alive. It's so easy — just play!

Design/ LoSiento

SEMILLA PERO NO SE TOCA

This project was commissioned by Badalona's Street Art Festival in 2009.

Since the themes were open, the idea was to move away from the usual spray paint and create an organic graffiti using adhesive spray and a vinyl template with the slogan "Semilla pero no se toca," making reference to the deforestation caused by humans in the past years.

All the graffiti is made out of grass. With the passage of time, it shrivels and changes color.

...HUN KINDEREN DOEN HET
BETER
OP SCHOOL...

...HUN GOLDEN
RETRIEVER
LAAT ZICHZELF UIT...

...DE BUURMAN HEEFT
EEN BETERE
BAAN...

...DE BUURVROUW IS
JONGER EN
MOOIER...

...EN HUN HUIS IS VAST
SNELLER
AFBETAALD
DAN HET MIJNE!

NIET ALLEEN
IS HET
GRAS
VAN DE BUREN
GROENER...

Design/ Autobahn
Client/ NRC Next

NRC NEXT MAGAZINE

Autobahn was asked by NRC Next to provide several articles with "typographic illustrations or illustrative typography." This assignment has resulted in vector illustrations, photographic solutions and a silver European Design Award in 2009 in the category "Book & Editorial Illustration."

"Bang voor de knal" ("Afraid of the Bang") is an article about a woman who, after having an accident with a child, has become too scared to drive a car again. Nowadays, nobody is completely free anymore. We all take our work to our homes or on holiday and don't seem to be able to relax at all. The article "Vrij van stand-by" ("Free of Stand-by") is in search of the possibilities revealed by an imagined "shut down" button. "Ja, schat..." ("Yes, dear...") gives insight to manipulation in relationships, plus tips and tricks. "Het gras van de buren..." ("The Neighbour's Grass...") is about mankind's envy and how our individual grudges against others' happiness will eventually wear us down as a society.

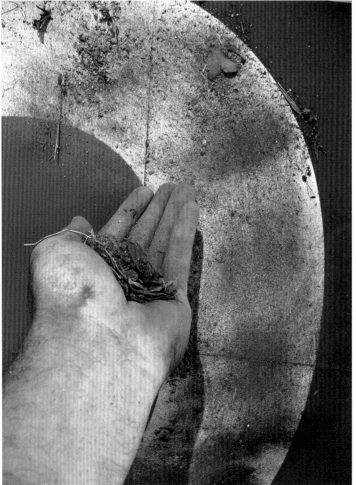

Design/ LoSiento

NON TOXIC

This project was commissioned by Badalona's Street Art Festival. The graffiti on the wall is composed entirely of the dirt collected from the ground outside the gallery. We used a vinyl template of the words "Non toxic nature," and added pulverized glue to make an adhesive graffiti phrase on which dirt would stick. This allowed the words to become visible.

Design/ Kasper Pyndt
Client/ Projektbuero Henkel.Hiedl

CHRISTMAS IS...

While working with Projektbuero Henkel. Hiedl in Berlin, Kasper was asked to design a Christmas calendar, using the medium of his choice. The only requirement was that the calendar had to be interactive. He started out by cutting out 24 long pieces of black fabric which represented the 24 days leading up to Christmas. Then he painted a unique word or sentence on each piece. These words are all alternate endings to the phrase "Christmas is..." The pieces of fabric were rolled up and firmly fixed to the ceiling in different "layers" so that the full depth of the room was accentuated. Each day in December, people could go into the room and pull a string attached to one of the rolls. A Christmas-related word unrolls and is revealed to the visitor.

Design/ LoSiento

XEMEI

Xemei is a Venetian food restaurant in Barcelona. Their main dish is the "nero di sepia" (spaghetti with squid ink). This inspired the whole identity project for the restaurant: the menus, business cards and logo have been done by finger painting with squid ink.

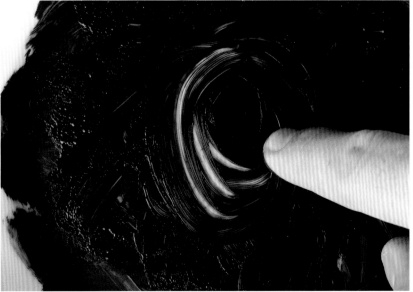

Design/ Elle Jeong Eun Kim
Client/ Self Initiated Work

TEMPORARY

I seek out my sense of belonging and existence through people, not by where I live. I lived half of my life bouncing between two homes: somewhere in the states and my birthplace, Seoul, Korea. Whether I am here or there I can't help but think everything around me is temporary. Sometimes I feel I belong in both places; sometimes I feel I belong in neither of these places. There is nothing we can identify as ultimately "what we really are" in our essential nature. We change and we are what we are in the context of the time in which we exist.

Design/ Victor Kay

TWISTED FIRESTARTER

To create this typeface each individual letter form was sculpted from metal wire. This skeleton was covered with tissue paper which was then soaked with lighter fluid. When lit with a match, the resulting inferno was captured at 5 frames a second with a high speed camera. Over 1,000 images were taken overall. To ensure consistent background lighting and safety the shoot was conducted outdoors in the early hours of the morning.

Around 50 photographs were captured for each individual character, providing massive variation in color and movement. An arduous editing process resulted in the most beautiful colors and shapes of flame being selected for the final letter forms. The resulting typeface has not been manipulated by software but is simply made up of the original photographs.

75

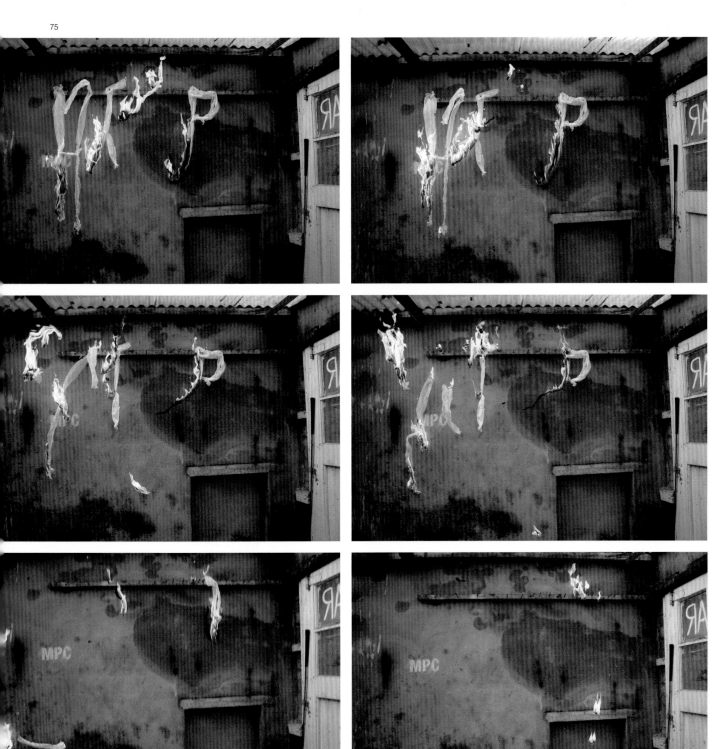

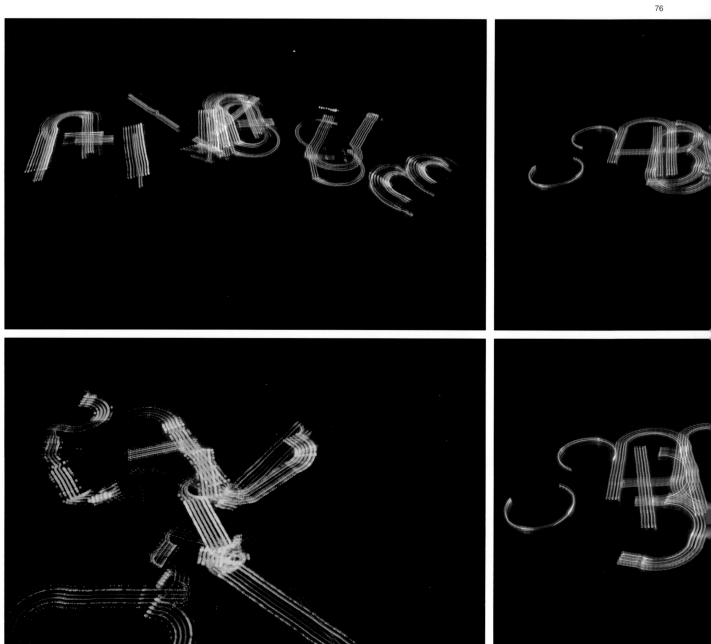

Design/ Ralph Hawkins
Client/ Self Initiated Work

AUTONOMOUS TYPEFACE

This was an attempt to create a system that interprets speech and
records it visually. The idea of the project was to capture some of
the subtlety lost when spoken language is transcribed. These images
are created using lyrics, and using the accompanying audio data
to dictate the appearance of the words.

Design/ Jozef Ondrík
Photograpy/ Martina Gajdačová

BÁRSHOCIČOHOKOL'VEK

Jozef created a visual identity for Bárshocičohokol'vek which was the title of an art show of typography. It showcases works from the graphic design studio of Tomas Bata University in Zlín (Czech Republic). The goal of this show is to introduce a new viewer to different treatments and concepts of typography. The exhibit does not have a common topic or theme and includes type composed of many different materials, which is basically the meaning of the title. This art show features Jozef Ondrík, Berjo Mouanga, Richard Jaros, Katerina Orlikova, Zdenek Kvasnica, Marek Suchanek and many more.

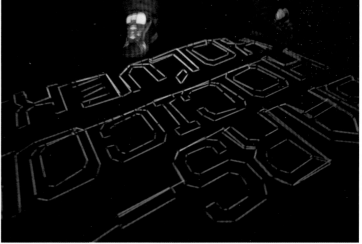

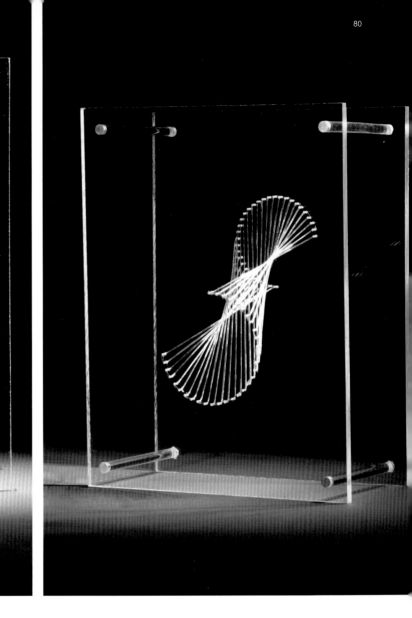

Design Agency/ Brian Banton
Design/ Brian Banton
Client/ School Project

HETEROSIS

The term "heterosis" refers to the increased size and fecundity of plants that results when different varieties of plants are crossbred. Recently, the term has been used to describe the benefits of both racial and cultural hybridity in contemporary society.

Each character in this kinetic typeface was designed by "blending" two (essentially one-dimensional) vector lines across a spatial plane, in order to produce a 3-D letter. The result is a set of characters that holds more possibilities than the standard two-dimensional alphabets to which we are accustomed.

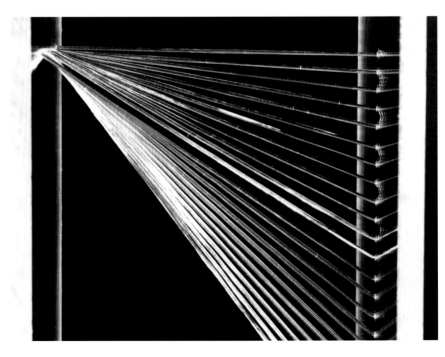

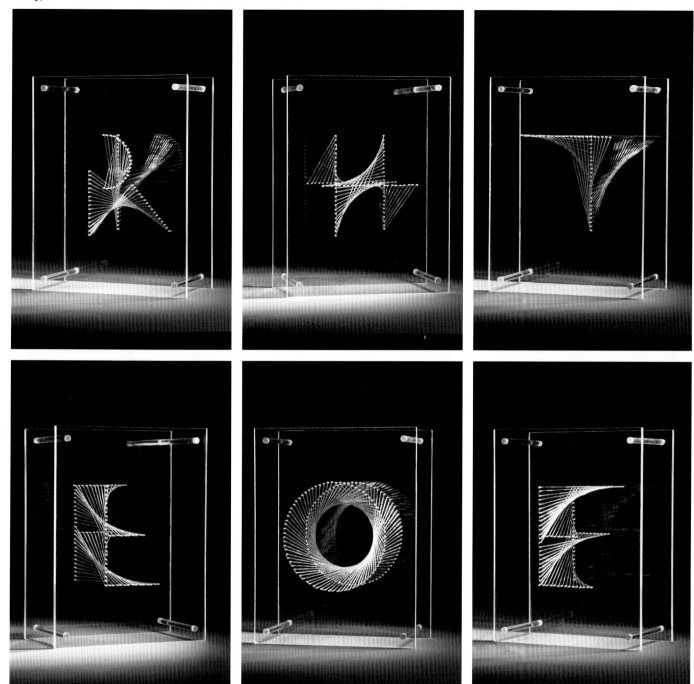

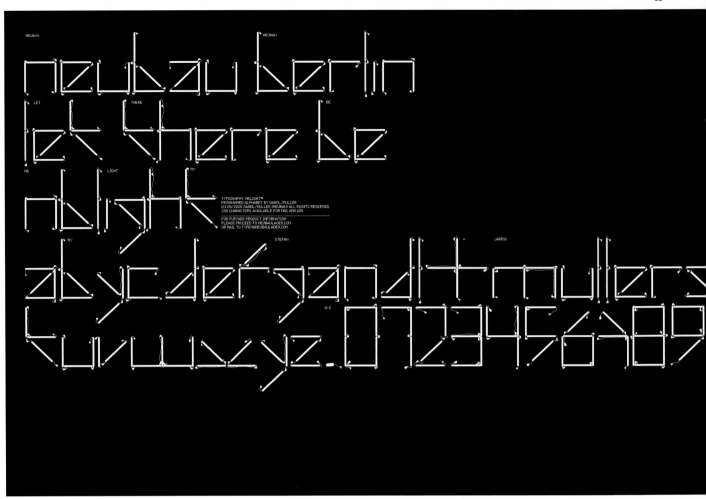

Design/ Jarrik Muller, Neubau

NB LIGHT

This typeface is the result of collaboration between Jarrik Muller and Neubau. They first made an installation with TL lights. After this analog version, they produced a digital version. The typeface was published in Neubau Modul.

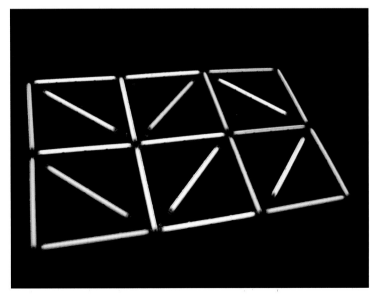

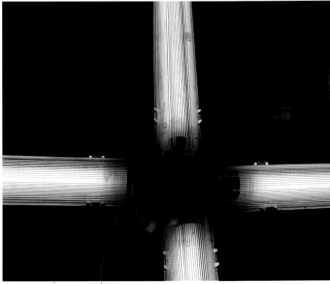

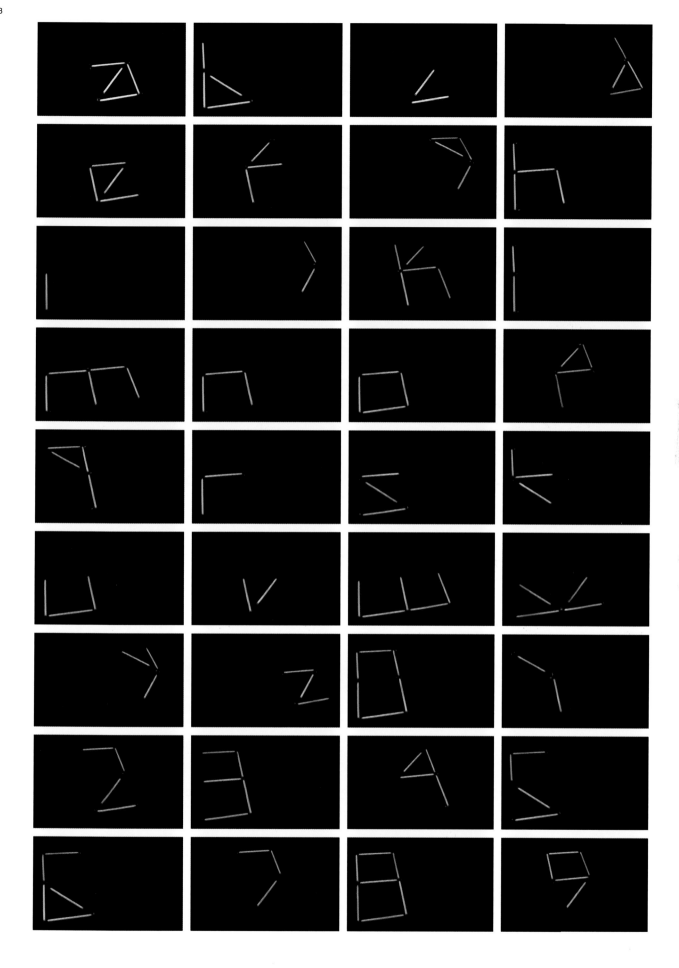

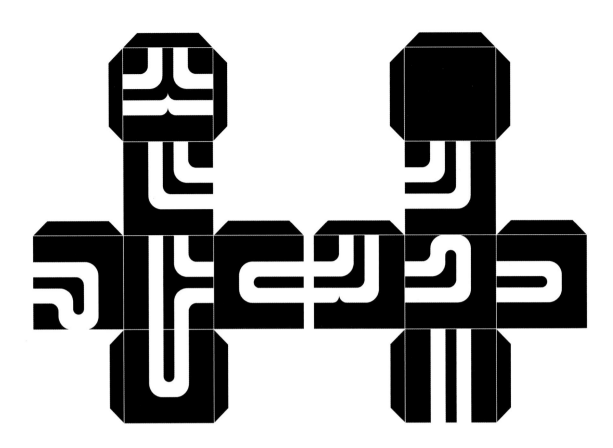

Design/ Jarrik Muller

BLOK TYPEFACE

The typeface is made out of blocks with a different form on each side. Six or nine of these blocks together creates a letter or number.

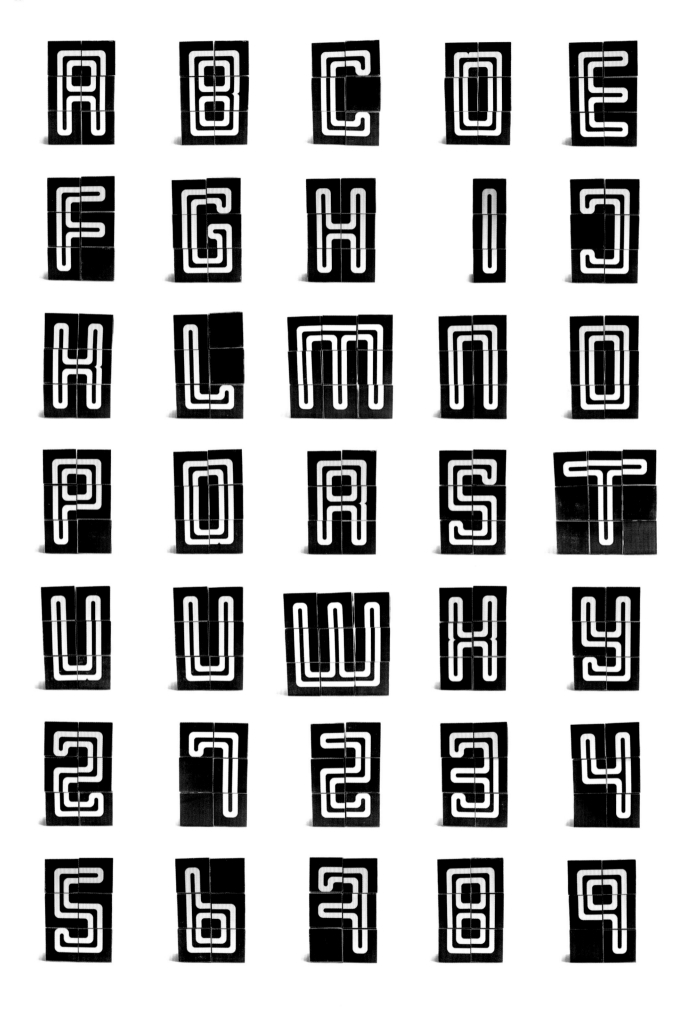

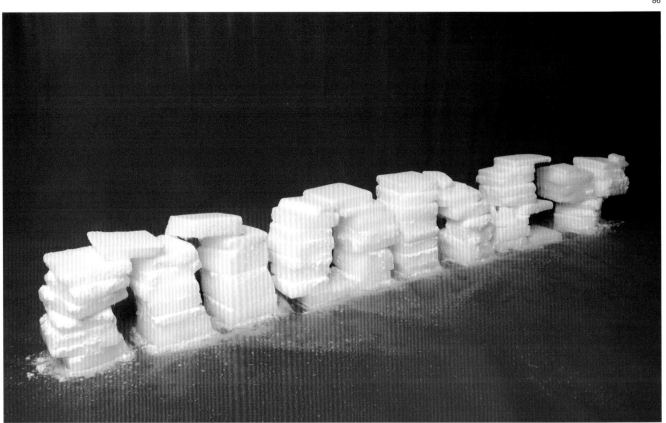

Design Agency/ Topos Graphics
Design/ Seth Labenz, Roy Rub
Client/ Topos Graphics
Photography/ Seth Labenz

DISAPPEARING ACT

This is an installment in our series of e-mailers — each focused
on the idea of money and bringing in new work. The MONEY
in this case was composed of dry ice. The performance had
us witnessing our own money disappearing into thin air.

Design Agency/ Raúl Iglesias
Design/ Raúl Iglesias
Photography/ Raúl Iglesias

ICE CUBE TYPE

The Ice Cube Type was created as part of a project called "Unfreezing ideas," aimed at representing ideas held in the mind which are eventually rejected and disappear. The "frozen" type became the core of the project in the form of melting ice cubes.

Design/ Ralph Hawkins
Client/ Self Initiated Work

WATERFORM TYPE

This typeface was an attempt to capture something
of the fleeting, ephemeral nature of language. Each
letter is unique and represents a moment in time.

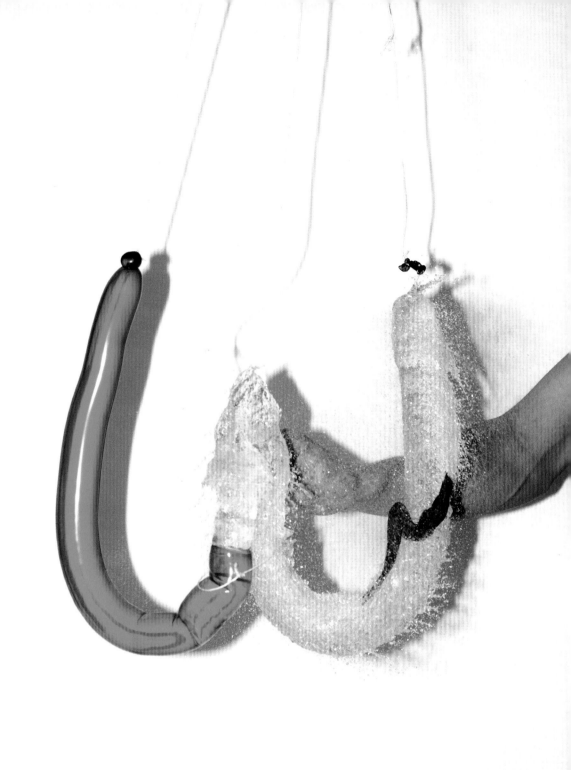

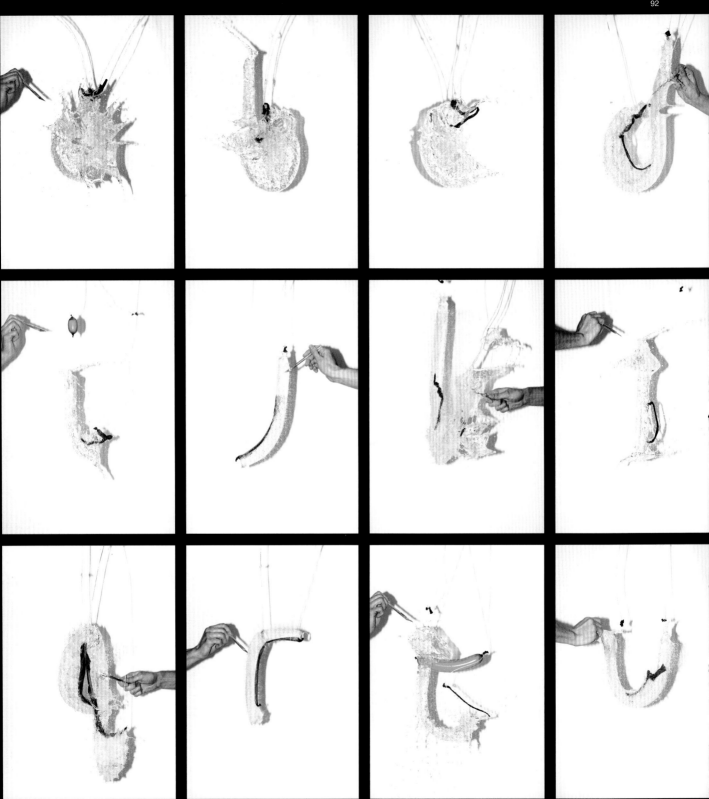

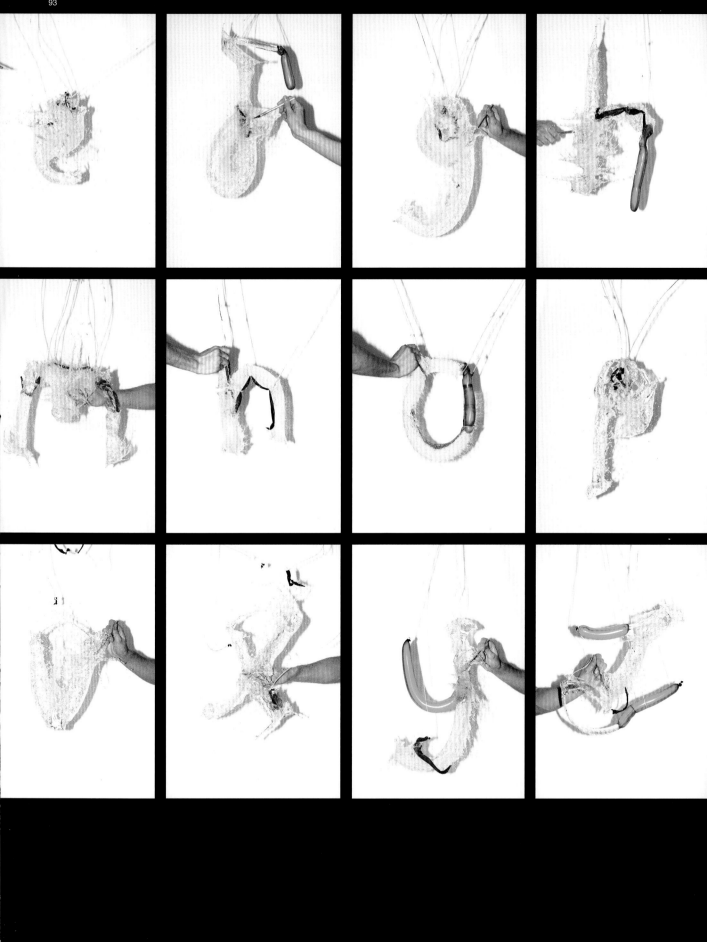

Design/ Juan Camilo Rojas

ENJOY

The piece was created using a word normally associated with and related to the brand being criticized and to a good feeling. The piece was created using over 18,000 nails spelling out the word "enjoy," which was then rusted using soda. Juan decided to use nails to counteract the positive feeling of the word "enjoy," creating an engaging visual contradiction which illuminates the health damage caused by drinking soda which is strong enough to rust the piece's nails.

Design/ Juan Camilo Rojas

POSI+IVO

Posi+ivo was created to target mainly young people and create awareness about the worldwide issue of STDs, which does not discriminate between race, ethnicity, gender or nationality. More than 2,800 condoms were placed on a 22" x 90" canvas. The black condoms, which surround the word "positivo," represent death and the negative aspects of this issue. The red condoms, which spell out the word "positivo," represent love, help, blood and the positive solutions of the problem. Juan decided to create this piece with the word Posi+ivo to capture, first, the positive attitudes of all young people regardless of their backgrounds. Second, condoms reflect safety or the lack of it. Posi+ivo can be seen from two different perspectives but as a whole advocates a positive attitude toward a sexually active lifestyle where people are aware of the risks of unsafe sex.

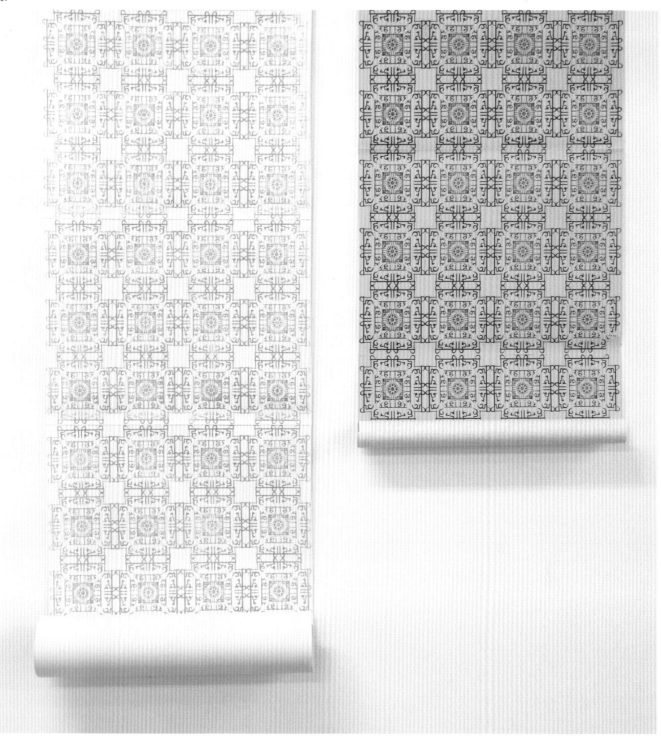

Design/ Nina Jua Klein
Client/ Self Initiated Work
Photography/ Nina Jua Klein

CURRY WALLPAPER

A cross-sensory wallpaper pattern created using elements of Indian typography and realized by screen printing using curry powder.

  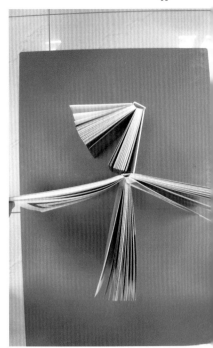

Design/ Erxu Chen

BOOKSTORE OF MOHEZI

All the visual identity of the bookstore is about books.
The design fulfills the goal of both consistent and
flexible applications. The aim is to present an infinite
world of books.

 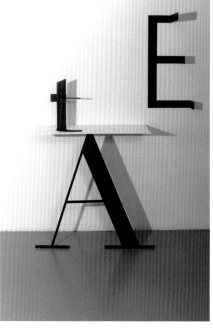 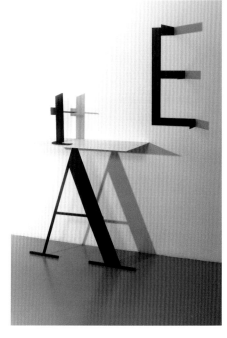

Design/ Iina Vuorivirta

THE MATTER OF SMALL THINGS COAT HANGER, SIDEBOARD, LAMP

Most readers aren't aware of the individual characters composing this sentence until someone draws attention to them. The device Iina Vuorivirta sometimes carries with her is a magnifying glass. Not because she has problems with her eyes, but because she is in love with details. Under a magnifying glass, the dullest of objects reveal characteristics hidden to the ordinarily blunt vision of humans. Lying on the floor with a magnifying glass in hand, the smooth floorboards are revealed to be a vast rugged landscape. Now Iina Vuorivirta is showing us what she sees. Her work consists of up-scaled three-dimensional metallic single letters. The formerly invisible letters stand on their own, with no need to justify their existence by any linguistic reference. After a while, the objects may even cease to be letters altogether and assume the form of abstract sculptures.

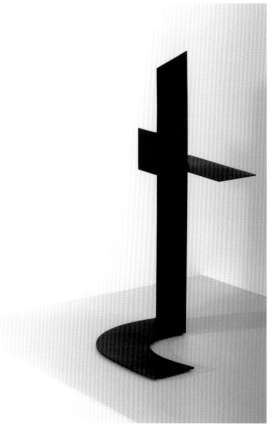 

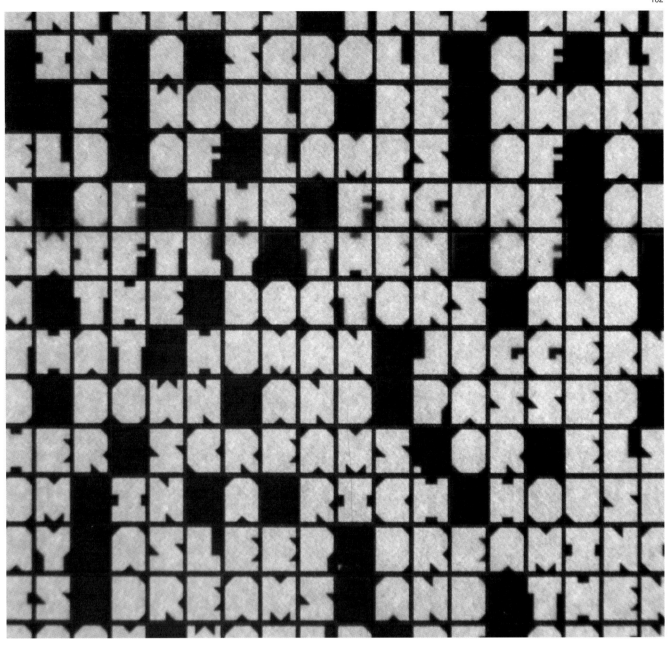

Design/ Nina Jua Klein

JEKYLL & HYDE

A typographic response to the interdependency of
Dr. Jekyll and Mr. Hyde in Robert Louis Stevenson's
The Strange Case of Dr. Jekyll and Mr. Hyde. The
mutual reliance of the two opposing characters in
the novella is imitated by utilizing a typeface's two
component parts: the form and its counter form
(negative space). The characters only become
legible when the two reliant layers in this piece
interact in the presence of light.

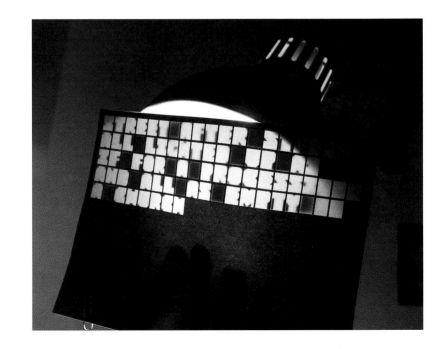

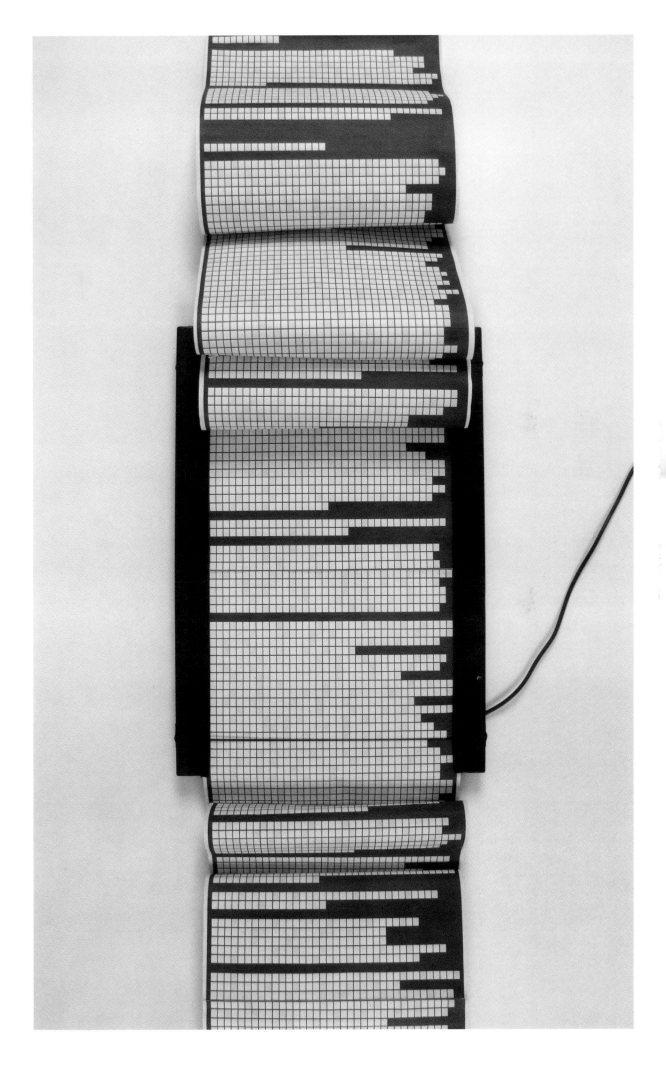

Design Agency/ Ethanissweet
Design/ Ethan Park & Ozgur Sezer
Illustration/ Ethan Park & Ozgur Sezer
Client/ Self Initiated Work
Photography/ Ethan Park & Ozgur Sezer

DON'T FEED

Public awareness motion clip.

Kingston University London
FACULTY OF ART, DESIGN & ARCHITECTURE
MA
GRADUATION
SHOW
MA ART & SPACE
MA COMMUNICATION DESIGN
MA CURATING CONTEMPORARY DESIGN
MA DESIGN : PRODUCT & SPATIAL
MA DIGITAL SET DESIGN
MA DRAWING AS PROCESS
MA FASHION DESIGN FOR INDUSTRY
MA ILLUSTRATION & ANIMATION
MA LANDSCAPE & URBANISM
MA PRODUCTION DESIGN FOR FILM & TV
MA SCREEN DESIGN FOR FILM & TV
HUNGER
Concept and design by Mina Lee and Young-Joon(Ethan) Park
PUBLIC VIEW
29 OCT - 02 NOV 2008
11 AM - 6 PM DAILY, ADMISSION FREE
BARGEHOUSE OXO TOWER WHARF,
BARGEHOUSE STREET, SOUTH BANK,
LONDON, SE1 9PH
www.kingston.ac.uk/atbargehouse
Bargehouse is an exciting atmospheric space in the heart of London's fast moving South Bank and Bankside areas. An untouched four-storey building, in its raw state Bargehouse is a blankcanvas with tremendous scope for exhibitions and events. Bargehouse is owned and managed by Coin Street Community Builders.
the.gallery@
OXO

Design Agency/ Ethanissweet
Design/ Ethan Park
Illustration/ Ethan Park
Client/ Self Initiated Work
Photography/ Ethan Park

MARRY ME PROJECT

Marry me project is an opportunity for me to communicate with the public audience in a simple, candid promotional way, in a manner that is more than casual. The intention behind this project is to reach beyond ourselves as individuals to make a difference by positive self-realization. With "Marry me," I created messages using the medium of self promotion advertising to spread a pure message about myself.

Design Agency/ Ethanissweet
Design/ Ethan Park
Client/ Self Initiated Work
Photography/ Ethan Park

CALLED HOME PROJECT

The project is about my feelings toward home and my childhood. For me, home refers to memories.

When I was young, my mother tried to keep me from crying by saying that if I cried, my dad would have to enter into military service. I was really worried my dad would have to do this — memories and stories like this compose my idea of home.

Design/ Jess Atkinson
Client/ Self Initiated Work
Photography/ Jess Atkinson

BUDDIES & BULLIES

Buddies & Bullies is a dedication to and celebration of emerging creative individuals. Based on the transition between student and professional identities, Buddies & Bullies highlights this major life transition in the art, illustration, and design community. Four words that haunt and encourage the young creative were personified: FEAR, OPPORTUNITY, PRESSURE & EXCITEMENT. Each word chosen encompasses the mystery and allure of the unknown. Buddies & Bullies interprets these words as characters discovering their own adventures.

Design Agency/ Happycentro
Design/ Federico Galvani
Illustration/ Andrea Manzati, Federico Galvani
Photography/ Federico Padovani + Monica Tarocco

NELLA MIA CITTÀ NESSUNO È STRANIERO

"Nella Mia Città Nessuno è Straniero (In My Town Nobody is a Stranger)" is a non-profit project created to promote the activities of a collective of associations that deal with cultural integration. Just as the various forms of individual letters grouped together create a nuanced language, different people with different histories and backgrounds can enrich the culture of a territory in a sign of tolerance theorized by Richard Florida.

Through workshops with informal groups and schools, we have made giant letters textured with used clothing provided by Caritas. Dozens of people have supported the initiative with their face on the poster for the campaign. The campaign is supported by CSV, a service center for volunteering.

Design Agency/ Happycentro
Design/ Giulio Grigollo
Illustration/ Giulio Grigollo
Photography/ Federico Padovani

SAY HELLO TO SANTA

Process:
1. Place the flour on the work surface, put the butter in the center and add 40g sugar and yolks. Knead vigorously until you get a soft and homogeneous mixture.

2. Roll out the dough about 1cm high and cut the letters into small biscuits.

3. Arrange on a plate lined with grease proof paper. Sprinkle with the remaining sugar.

4. Bake in a hot oven at 150-160°C until the biscuits are lightly golden.

5. Take out of the oven and serve hot.

Poster ingredients:
Flour, 225g; Butter, 150g; Sugar, 50g; Eggs, 3 egg yolks.

Ingredients:
Flour, 225 g • Butter, 150 g • Sugar, 50 g • Eggs, 3 yolk eggs.

Happycentro – "Say hello to Santa."
www.happycentro.it
info@happycentro.it

Design Agency/ Happycentro
Design/ Federico Galvani

MOZAMBIQUE TOY SOLDIER TYPOGRAPHY

The traveling art show collective is a fund-raising drive for ASEM, a non-profit organization that helps the children of Mozambique. This exhibition will consist of various works of art and a small photography section consisting of a compilation of Mozambican images that are given to artists as inspiration.

The intent of Imagining Mozambique is to create thought provoking art that will draw attention to the day-to-day life of the children of Mozambique. Furthermore, Happycentro hopes the exhibition will open up a broader conversation in the media about the situation for children in Mozambique and ideally inspire people to act in one form or another. This project is made with the support of: Jamie N Kim, Mo Manager and Wieden+Kennedy.

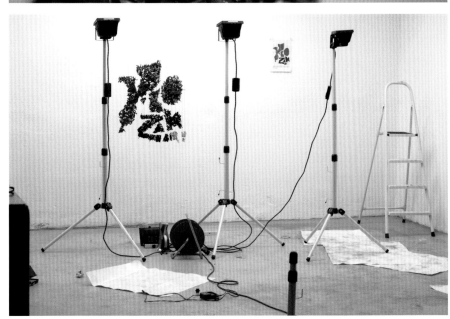

Mozambique, officially the Republic of Mozambique (Portuguese: Moçambique or República de Moçambique), is a country in southeastern Africa bordered by the Indian Ocean to the east, Tanzania to the north, Malawi and Zambia to the northwest, Zimbabwe to the west and Swaziland and South Africa to the southwest. It was explored by Vasco da Gama in 1498 and colonized by Portugal in 1505. By 1510, the Portuguese had virtual control of all of the former Swahili sultanates on the east African coast. From about 1500, Portuguese trading posts and forts became regular ports of call on the new route to the east. Mozambique became independent in 1975, to which it became the People's Republic of Mozambique shortly after, and **was the scene of an intense civil war from 1977 to 1992**. The country is a member of the Community of Portuguese Language Countries and the Commonwealth of Nations and an observer of the Francophonie. Mozambique (Moçambique) was named by the Portuguese after Msumbiji, the Swahili name of Mozambique Island and port-town. Mozambique's life expectancy and infant mortality rates are both among the worst ranked in the world. Its Human Development Index is one of the lowest on earth.

Wikipedia — The Free Encyclopedia
Federico Galvani — Happycentro — Italy — 2009
Photography by Federico Padovani

Design/ Therese Vandling
Client/ Self Initiated Work
Photography/ Therese Vandling

AND GOD SAID

A typeface inspired by Isaac Newton's theories on light and color.

Design/ LoSiento

THE PINKER TONES

It is a volumetric font made with porex and mirror surface.
The typography was created for the band The Pinker Tones'
new album.

Art direction/ Designpolitie, Eric Wie
Design/ Autobahn
Client/ Self Initiated Work

TAPE WRITER

Rationale behind the project's execution: Tape writer is a font based upon the grid of fences. It's a form of graffiti that makes optimal use of its carrier. Tape writer is for everyone who has a passionate opinion and the urge to express it in public — in this case, with a roll of tape.

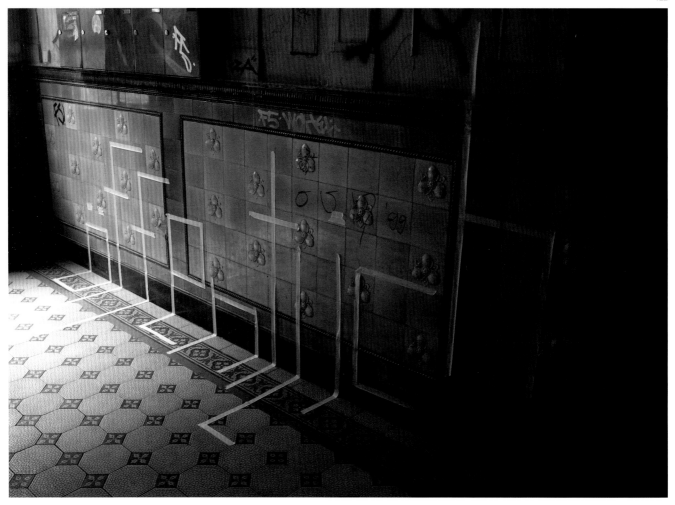

Design/ Johanna Hullár

INSIDE-OUT

Take your clothes off, bring your life out to the street, let everybody in, your life is inside-out.

S-EEE is a self-organized group of artists and students working with the frontier of photography and typography. Originally based at the University of Kaposvar, Hungary, and led by Lajos Major, it now has an international scope comprised of artists and creators from France, Denmark, the United States, and Iceland.

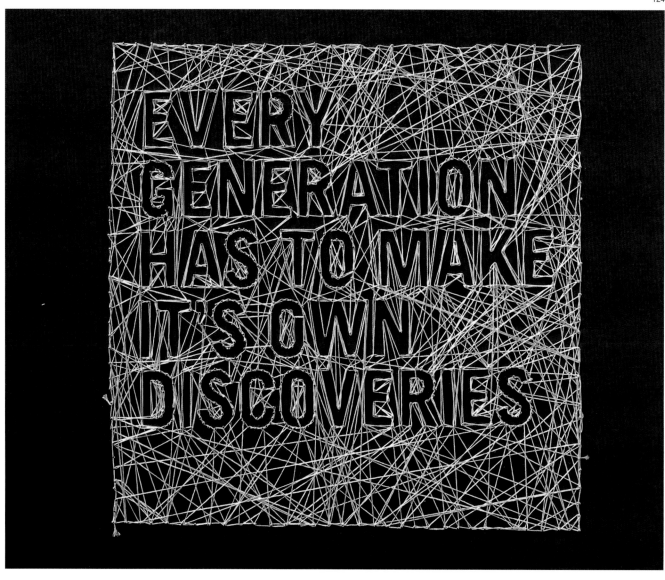

Design Agency/ Me Studio
Design/ Martin Pyper

GENERATIONS

A typographical illustration made entirely by hand using thousands of steel pins and 100 meters of kite string. The text is a quote by Milton Glaser, a favorite of Martin's. The designer chose to make the piece using the philosophy behind the quote itself... not planning ahead, but instead discovering how it worked as he went along. It was eventually used as a double-page magazine spread and he later created a large-format poster too.

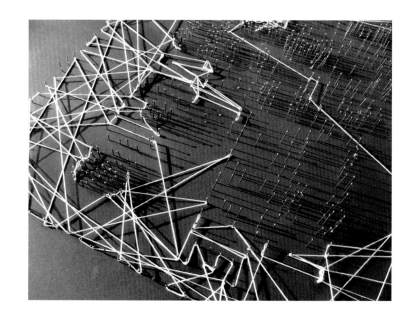

Design/ Elle Jeong Eun Kim
Client/ Self Initiated Work

SEED AND FRUIT

I exist through relationships I have with people I encounter in my life — not because I am myself. We weave in and out of each other's lives. We are all interconnected. Every event, including our perceptions, behavior, decisions, and actions is causally determined by an unbroken chain of events. When any link is broken, all the other links are affected. I see this piece as a map of my existence. It's woven from the memories of my past relationships and the relationships I have now. I started with a single thread and I continue to add the threads of others. I weave, unravel, weave and make a knot.

Design/ Dominic Liu, Duc Tran, Stefan Spec
Creative Director/ Kyosuke Nishida
Art Directors/ Brain Li, Sean Yendrys

STILL LIFE COMES ALIVE

This project was a unique life-sized typographical installation made up of thousands of pieces of paper assembled together. The folds and shapes formed the sentence "STILL LIFE COMES ALIVE," bringing to life my concept of a typographic paper sculpture. It was a long-cherished idea I had, and I finally had the opportunity to make it come true with a great team of collaborators, for the Concordia University End of Year exhibition in 2010.

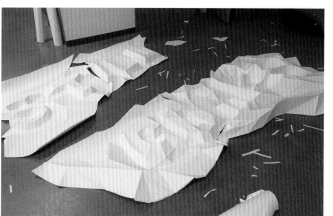

Design/ Gluekit
Client/ Print Magazine
Photography/ Gluekit

PRINT MAGAZINE COVER AND SPREADS

Gluekit created the cover and eight interior pages for *Print Magazine*'s Regional Design Annual. The issue, published annually, features the best design from across the United States, divided by region. The Gluekit designers were asked to create a spread for each geographic region as well as a cover that synthesized the individual spreads. Gluekit built the letterforms from wood and felt. They composed the simple three-dimensional bright shapes into letterforms that spelled out each region's name, inserting themselves into each composition in order to reflect the relationship between designer and material in the design process while utilizing photographic perspective. This project was conceived as a way to magnify the design process at a human scale.

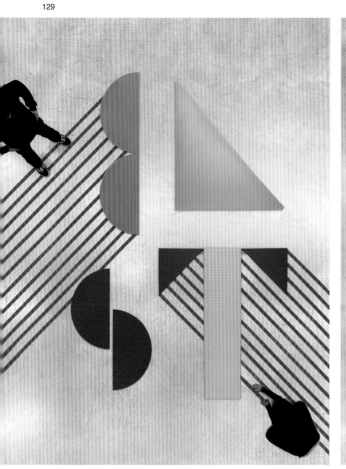

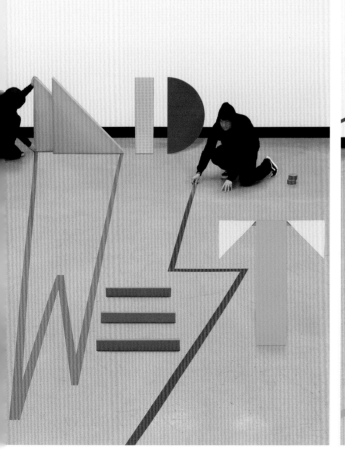

Art Direction/ Stefan Sagmeister
Design/ Richard The
Photography/ Photo Courtesy of Tom Powel and Deitch Projects

DEITCH NOTEBOOK WALL

Sagmeister Inc. incorporated the title of their show at Deitch projects in New York's Soho into a wall of open notebooks, inviting the visitors to write their own "Things they have learned in their life" using the supplied pencils hanging from the ceiling.

How did you get started designing type?

As a graphic designer, it is my job to communicate a message through the means of either type or image — or both. As I started to become familiar with certain typefaces, I began finding myself more and more interested in the art of typography. My numerous exploits in the field of type design were a result of this fascination.

What inspires you most? Are there any typography designers or movements that you find particularly inspiring?

Although I do keep my eye trained for any strokes of typographical genius that may be floating about, I don't draw inspiration form any one typographer. My sources of inspiration are usually drawn from seeing something in the street, stumbling upon something in a magazine, or listening to music. For direct inspiration by what is out there at the moment, you can't look any further than the internet.

Take the example of your photo illustration manipulation and type design in the self-initiated project "Block Noise." How does photography interact with typeface design in your work?

Having come from a background of both typography and photography, a lot of the photographic images found in my work are self-produced. This enables me to capture the right shots required in order to complement all aspects of the project, including the type design. Take Block Noise. The type design itself is an experiment with space and simplicity. These qualities are also immediately apparent throughout the interior gallery and exterior landscape images I generated.

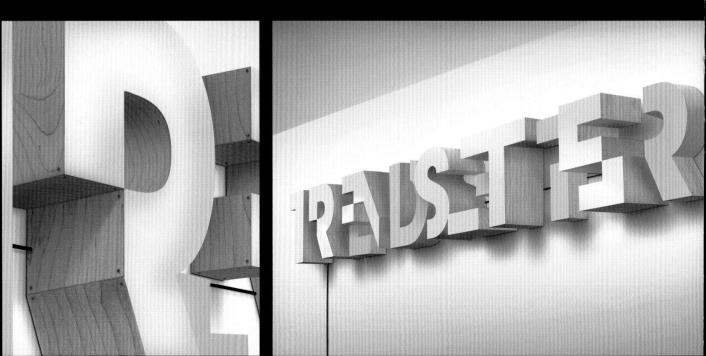

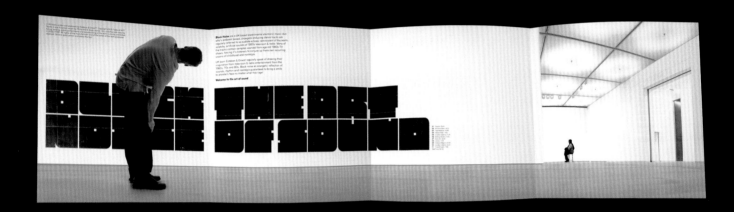

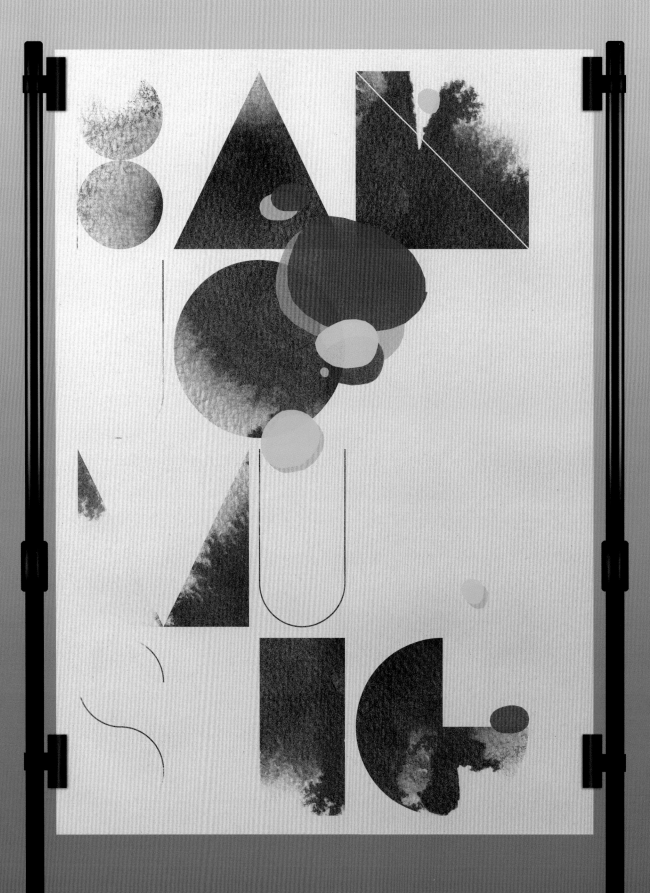

"Most of the time, we use the same grid in the typeface design for the other designed items, in order to create a visual coherence between all of the communication elements."

Interview with
TWOPOINTS

How did you get started designing type?

We studied at the Royal Academy of Art in The Hague, which is famous for type education. We do not consider ourselves type designers, though. The typefaces we create are all part of a graphic design project. Most of the time, we use the same grid in the typeface design for the other designed items, in order to create a visual coherence between all of the communication elements.

What inspires you most? Are there any typographic designers or movements that you find particularly inspiring?

The project itself, the product or identity, is what inspires us most. We always start by defining the communication strategy of the visual communication first. The typeface or design is then just a logical next step.

For the project with Banjo Music, what was your favourite part of the design process? How important is the design of the typeface in leading to the success of the visual identity of Banjo Music?

We are still working for Banjo Music and the visual system allows us to create new applications all the time. It is great to have developed a flexible visual system that works well as a visual identity, but also never bores you when you have to develop something new. The system has a good balance between diversity and coherence.

The typeface appears now and then, but the corporate elements are most important. They make the visual identity recognizable. The visual identity is very successful in that sense. People remember the visual identity, plus they like it and all that without a logo. So you can consider it a success for the client, because he is remembered, as well as a success for us, because we were able to break with the traditional logo system.

BANJO MUSIC
C/CONSELL DE CENT, 236 PPAL 2ª
08011 BARCELONA
E   INFO@BANJOMUSIC.ES
T   +34 934 517 072

BANJO MUSIC
C/CONSELL DE CENT, 236 PPAL 2ª
08011 BARCELONA
E   INFO@BANJOMUSIC.ES
T   +34 934 517 072

BANJO MUSIC
C/CONSELL DE CENT, 236 PPAL 2ª
08011 BARCELONA
E   INFO@BANJOMUSIC.ES
T   +34 934 517 072

BANJO MUSIC
C/CONSELL DE CENT, 236 PPAL 2ª
08011 BARCELONA
E   INFO@BANJOMUSIC.ES
T   +34 934 517 072

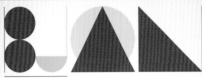

BANJO MUSIC
C/CONSELL DE CENT, 236 PPAL 2ª
08011 BARCELONA
E   INFO@BANJOMUSIC.ES
T   +34 934 517 072

BANJO MUSIC
C/CONSELL DE CENT, 236 PPAL 2ª
08011 BARCELONA
E   INFO@BANJOMUSIC.ES
T   +34 934 517 072

BANJO MUSIC
C/CONSELL DE CENT, 236 PPAL 2ª
08011 BARCELONA

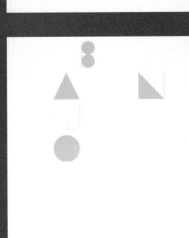

BANJO MUSIC
C/CONSELL DE CENT, 236 PPAL 2ª
08011 BARCELONA

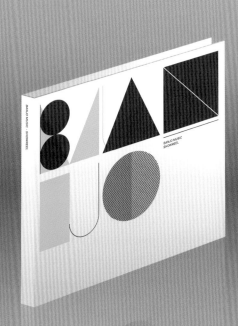

Interview with
SIXSTATION WORKSHOP

How did you get started designing type?

When I first started my design work, I was kind of lost, as I just created by copying others' ideas without my own style. I could draw excellent replications of existing styles, but couldn't capture the soul of the ideas until I heard a foreign designer talking about the close relationship between life and creativity. I realized I have to choose elements that are found in my life and create things representative of my reality. So designing type is another way of building my own style. I believe that unique typographic design lasts longer than most graphic design.

What inspires you the most? Are there any typographic designers or movements that you find particularly inspiring?

Actually my cultural background and things happening around me and in my life inspire me the most. No particular one can be named.

You take on quite a lot of fashion related projects. Take the fashion brand FAYTE as an example. How do you express its personality and uniqueness through typography? Have you thought of using the alphabet instead of Chinese characters in the design process?

FAYTE is about exploring the relationship between the world and our lives. The Chinese character of FAYTE is combined with two words: one is about fatalism and the other one is about randomness. When two words are combined, it represents life. This is the power and style of my typeface — it is readable but at the same time meaningful.

The reason I use Chinese characters in my design is simple: it's about the confirmation of one's own identity. Knowing who you are, where you are from, and which way you are going is a very important point for a good designer.

"The reason I use Chinese characters in my design is simple: it's about the confirmation of one's own identity. Knowing who you are, where you are from, and which way you are going is a very important point for a good designer."

_IF EVERY ONE CAN SHARE
THIS IS NO STRANGER

_PEACE WITH LOVE

_TO THE WORLD

_START FROM US

菩提
本無樹

Design/ Nod Yound

THE PUTI TREE

This work is a typographic interpretation of two poems quoted from the
original Zen classic, *The Platform Sutra of the Sixth Patriarch*, which dates back
almost 1,500 years. Nod Young uses his understanding of Zen philosophy to
understand the ability to create: dust is an obstacle to creativity, and while
you can of course eliminate all external interference to ensure that your works
maintain the greatest sense of purity, if you choose to forget about being tied
down by rules, how is it possible to feel interference?

明鏡
亦非臺

本來
無一物

何處
惹塵埃

Design/ Wing Lau

I AM INFORMATIVE

"I am Informative" is an experimental / flexible sign system design proposal for the specialised design bookstore Published Art, located in Surry Hills, Sydney.

The entire sign system was named "I am Informative." The design of the sign system aims to solve the communication problems of a store that is operated by a single staff person. Sharon, the sole owner of the store, enjoys sharing her knowledge of titles with customers, according to what they are interested in. However, verbal communication difficulties sometimes occur when there is more than one customer in the store.

The design of the information system responds to the specific graphic structure and characteristics of the space, and results in a harmonious existence of the signage with the bookstore environment. The incorporation of the store's pre-existing graphic identity, the multi-layered historical aspect of the site location, and the idea of highlighting while reading a book were key components that made up the conceptual framework of the design.

ABCDEFG
HIJKLMN
OPQRSTU
VWXYZ

ABCDEFG
HIJKLMN
OPQRSTU
VWXYZ ×'

PUBLISHED
ARCHITECTURE ×

PUBLISHED
ILLUSTRATIONS ×

PUBLISHED
GRAPHICS ×

PUBLISHED
PHOTOGRAPHY ×

PUBLISHED
JOURNAL ×

PUBLISHED OBJECT ×

I'M A
PRIZE WINNER ×

I AM A
BEST SELLER ×

BAD COVER
GREAT CONTENT ×

I'M RECOMMENDED
BY SHARON ×

I AM HELPFUL ×

BOOK OF
THE WEEK ×

BOOK OF
THE MONTH ×

BACK IN STOCK ×

BACK IN PRINT ×

LATEST EDITION ×

I AM INSPIRING ×

I'VE JUST ARRIVED ×

**NATURE
REVISITED**
21.09. – 13.10.2007

**TORNO SUBITOT
(ATTO II)**
26.10. – 17.11.2007

WELSCHLAND
23.11. – 15.12.2007

**(HIBK)
HAD I BUT KNOWN?**
HAUS AM GERN
24.10. – 22.11.2008

HEIMATPÄCKLI
ADAM TELLMEISTER
06.12. – 20.12.2008

**...THEN WE TAKE
BERLIN PART. 2**
11.01. – 16.02.2008

ANA STRIKA
22.02. – 29.03.2008

MARC BAUER
04.04. – 10.05.2007

**ISABELLE
KRIEG**
27.02. – 09.04.2009

**DON'T FOLLOW ME,
I'M LOST TOO**
17.04. – 30.05.2009

**ZU GAST BEI
VERLIERERN**
16.05. – 14.06.2008

A.I.R. ONE
ARTISTS IN RESIDENCE
20.06. – 26.07.2008

SPUREN. WACHSEN.
ERIC HENR AURELIO KOPAINIG
12.09. – 18.10.2008

**DOPPELTER
BODEN**
09.01. – 21.02.2009

A.I.R. TWO
ARTISTS IN RESIDENCE
05.06. – 18.07.2009

Design Agency/ onlab
Art Direction/ Nicolas Bourquin, Thibaud Tissot
Design/ Thibaud Tissot

SUBSTITUT

Substitut is a non-profit exhibition space with the objective of presenting Swiss artists in Berlin. The name of the space is drawn from the words "subculture" and "institute" — indicating the gallery's mixed nature. onlab's main principle for the corporate identity was to play with typography in a non-Swiss way, i.e. free as opposed to strict, and playful as opposed to formal. As the interior ot the space is designed to be unfinished, with crude walls which reveal the space's authentic past, the typography is also built on two layers: only when carefully studied do the two layers reveal the content of the exhibition. The actions of decoding and unveiling suggest Substitut's unfinished and emerging nature.

ABCDEFGHIJKLM
NOPQRSTUVWXYZ

PLAIN

ABCDEF
GHIJKL
MNOPQR
STUVWX
YZ

Design/ Zaijia Huang

ESPACE ALBERT CAMUS

This project is the creation and implementation of all communication media within the 09/10 season. It was produced in collaboration with Sophie Raynaud.

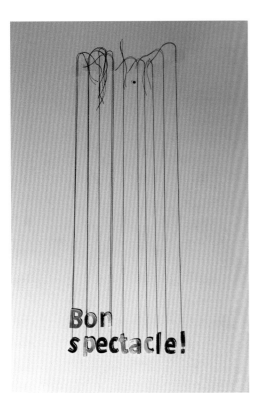

Design/ Farina Kuklinski

PLAY.

"Play" was my final graduation project for the Academy of Fine Arts Maastricht in the Netherlands.

Working with real things in a three-dimensional space allows me to minimize the actual distance between myself and the object. This happens without any computer support. In my opinion, design feels more realistic and alive this way; it can be slightly inaccurate, but in a good way. This adds a sense of ease to my work. Handmade things show imperfections; this happens accidentally or as a result of experimentation. It is simply the side effect of having fun and playing around. Through hand-produced projects, the designer becomes involved with the image and becomes a vivid part of it. I believe design is all about fun. Play is the beginning of every invention, and it's how we learn. Play helps children learn to be adults by exploring the world, and it's how we feel alive. It's so easy — just play!

Design/ Anton Gridz
Photography/ Anton Gridz

COLOR LINES FONT

From time to time I come up with interesting ideas, which I would love to put into reality. I had a mental image of nice letters of different thicknesses in my head. Once, I was on a train and the idea of creating a decorative font from parts with different thicknesses came to me. When I came home, the first thing I did was sit at my computer and create the first 9 symbols. The next day, I drew the rest of the symbols to create a complete font. The letters came out to be "alive" and bright, which attracts attention. I would gladly create a Nike commercial using this font, or, if necessary, create a completely new font. I hope one day I will be able to "just do it!"

A B C D E F
G H I J K L
M N O P Q R
S T U V W X
Y Z 1 2 3 4
5 6 7 8 9 0
? ! + - , .

Design/ Therese Vandling
Illustration/ Therese Vandling
Client/ Skin magazine
Photography/ Ram Shergill

A-Z OF FASHION

A collaboration between Therese Vandling and photographer Ram Shergill for Skin magazine.

Design Agency/ NAM
Design/ Takayuki Nakazawa
Photography/ Hiroshi Manaka

D, R, E, A, M

This is another version of "Kids Alphabet" that uses the same method as applied to fashion photography. It is photographed by the digital scanner camera "BETTERLIGHT." The typography is formed by the trace of the movement of the object or the model within the area that the camera is able to record.

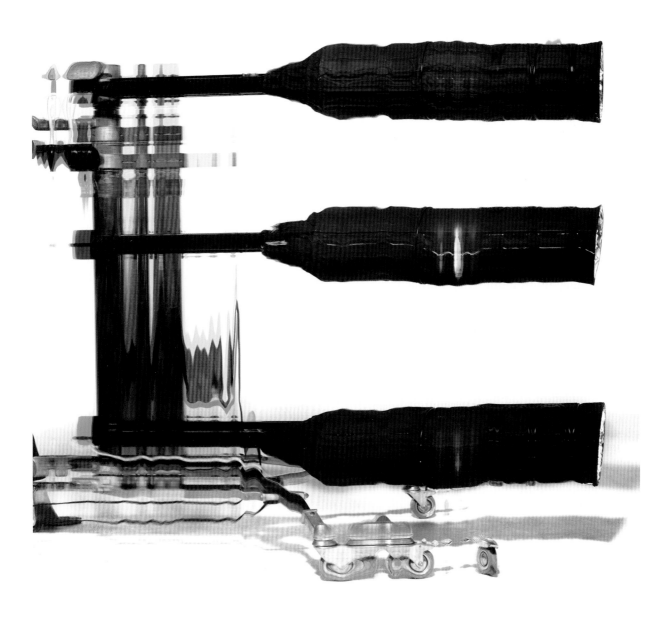

Design Agency/ Ken-tsai Lee Image Design Company
Design/ Ken-tsai Lee
Illustration/ Ken-tsai Lee
Client/ Taiwan designers' web

TAIWAN DESIGNERS' WEEK 2010

Designers always care about life, environment and new trends. The theme
of 2010 Taiwan Designers Week was "Care." Continuing with the TWDW
core spirit, "share and enjoy," 2010 Taiwan Designers Week focused on how
designers care about different aspects of the world. The roots of caring are
seeing, listening, understanding, and implementing generosity and support by
using practical methods, in order to make the world a better place.

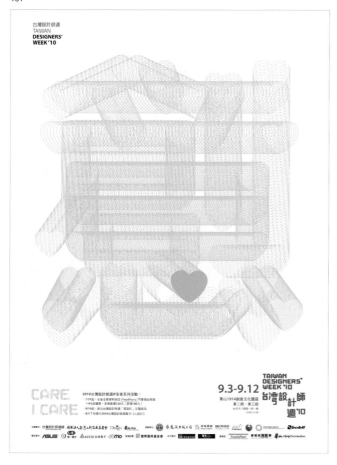

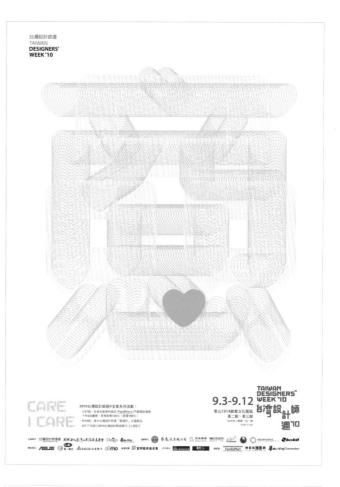

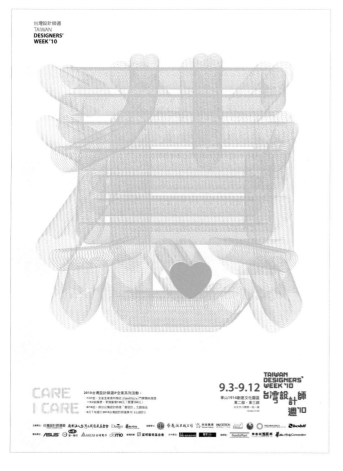

Design Agency/ Hellyeee
Design/ Ferdi Alıcı

CALLOSAL APRAXIA

A temporal analysis of a 43-year-old woman who suffered a spontaneous corpus callosum disconnection which resulted in apraxia and apraxic agraphia confined to the left hand provided support for Liepmann's (Liepmann, 1900; Liepmann and Maas, 1907) hypothesis that there is a centre for visuokinaesthetic (space-time) engrams in the left hemisphere of right-handed patients that controls skilled motor acts in either hand. The patient's recovery also allowed us a better understanding of the mechanisms underlying various types of apraxia.

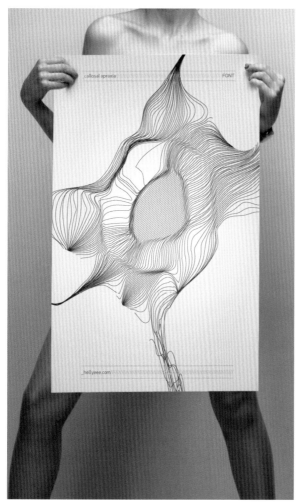

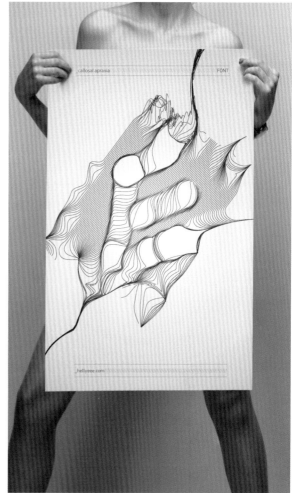

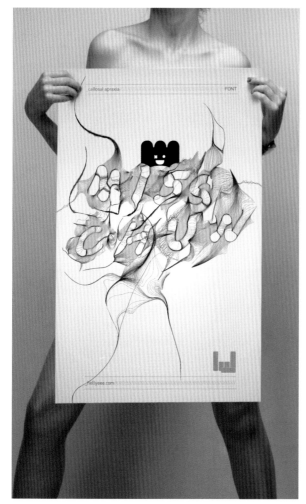

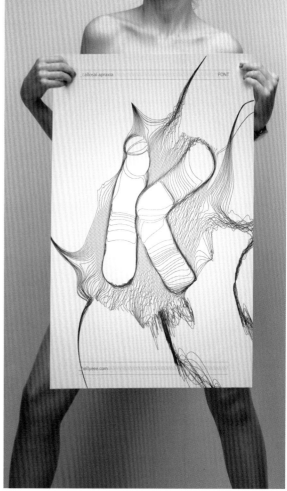

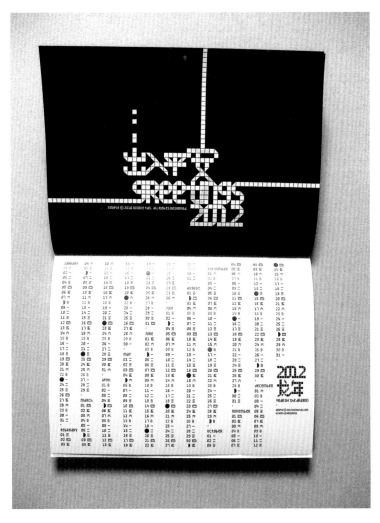

Design/ WINNIE TAN

THE SIMPLE FONT

The original concept of the Simple Font was that it should be somewhat pixel-based. I came up with the idea at the beginning of 2010, and the drawings were created in April during my convalescence. Richard Dawkin's Selfish Gene played a big part in influencing my view of the font as a game of successful replicated strokes that can be manipulated into various forms. The Simple Font began with the alphabet, to which a series of icons was introduced, followed by an avalanche of Chinese characters. The usage of Chinese characters was loosely determined by the lunar calendar. In a nutshell, the Simple Font is a single-weight, minimal, grid-based San-serif font. Prudent with details and sturdy in form, the geometric structure marks the foundation of a cross-cultural assortment of Latin alphabets, Chinese characters, and thematic icons. After months of extensive typesetting, the Simple Font is well-polished for use in graphic design, game design, information design, logotypes, advertisements, and headlines.

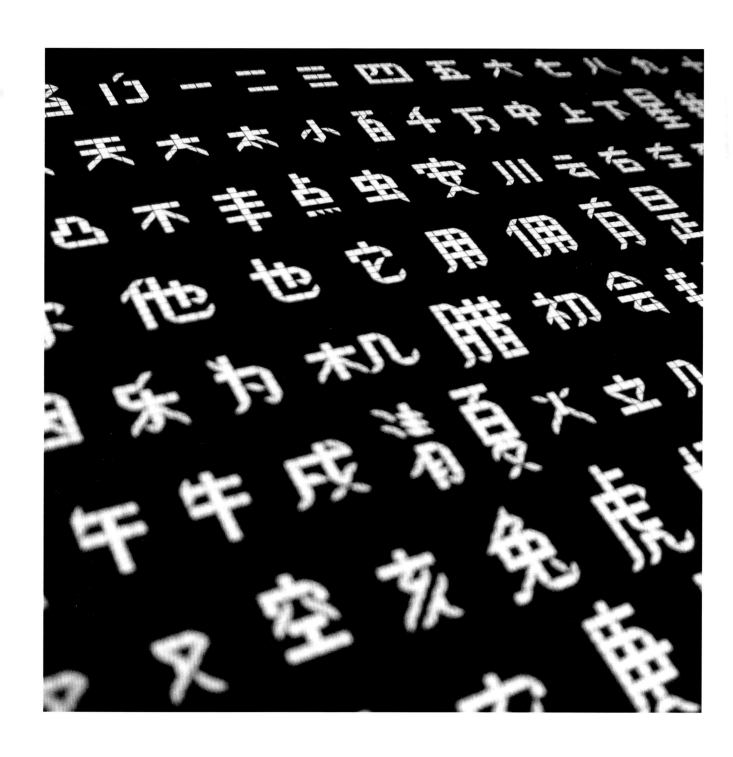

MAN JIANG HONG

A new inspection and embellishment of traditional
Chinese culture to make it attractive to the
younger generation.

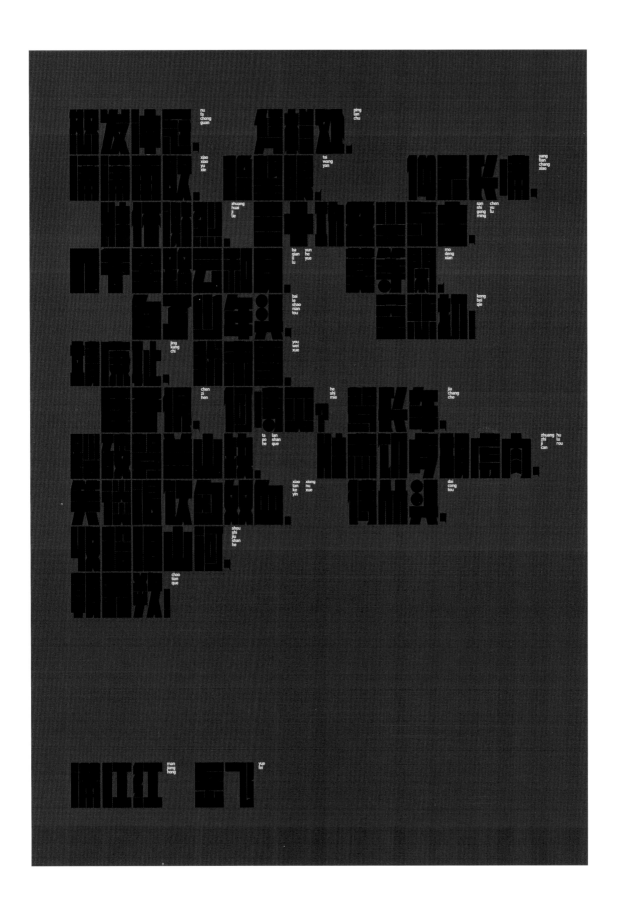

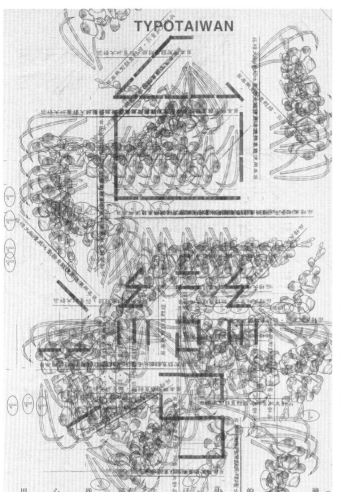

Design/ Wei Cheng Chu

TYPO TAIWAN

The red and white plastic bag is a common object of daily life in Taiwan. Wei Cheng Chu wanted to utilize an essential but under-utilized aspect of Taiwan's image, so he chose this item as the foundation material in his creation of a typeface for Taiwan. He believes the most beautiful things are unique to each individual's everyday life.

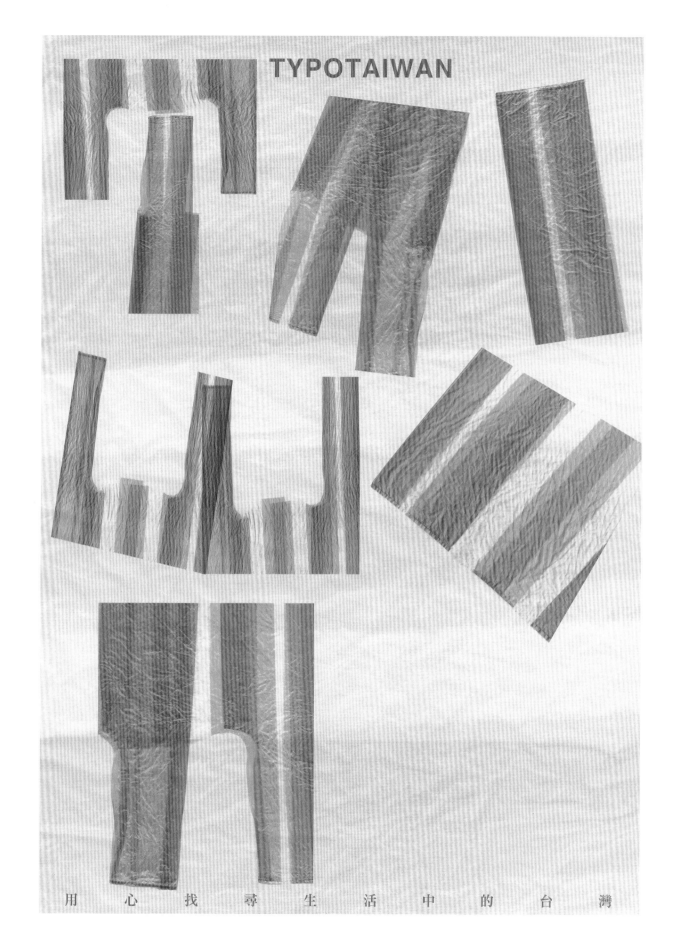

TYPOTAIWAN

用 心 找 尋 生 活 中 的 台 灣

The Eight
Principles
of Yong

Design/ Wei Cheng Chu

THE EIGHT PRINCIPLES OF YONG

The Eight Principles of Yong is a philosophy in Chinese calligraphy.
After deconstruction and reorganization, a new typeface is
created between east and west.

FAYTE
Life and Number . Number and Life

Design/ Sixstation Workshop

LIFE WITH NUMBER, NUMBER WITH LIFE

The project is all about introspection and examination of destiny and one's own life. Within thousands of lives, there are millions of possibilities.

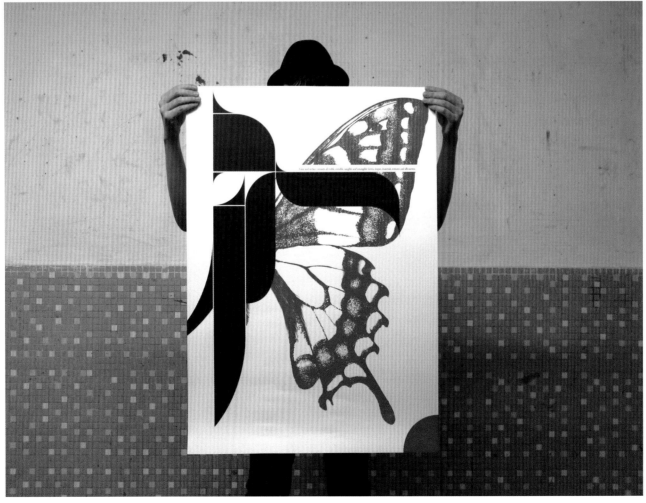

Design Agency/ Disinlok
Design/ Chan Ka Lok Casper
Client/ Self Initiated Work
Photography/ Chan Ka Lok Casper

HUMAN CONNECTION

To live is to understand the essence of life. These three posters propose and unify a personal view of communicative life through graphic means. Through the integration of single points (individual people who create) to line surfaces (the medium of expression), the space (or sky) becomes an expanse of possibility. This holistic series signifies a personal view of conceptual expression through visual communication.

Sky: A space embraces mystical myths and idiosyncratic unpredictability. It is a metaphysical state of mind, an origin of cyclic life and infinite aspiration.

Medium: A line and surface connects all visible, invisible, tangible and intangible forms, shapes, materials, textures and silhouettes.

People: A wealth of varied communication emerges, acting as a source of wisdom, exploration, and information propagation.

Design Agency/ Studio mw
Design/ Studio mw
Client/ Self Initiated Work

5QUANT4

Project 5QUANT4 is based on graphic and typographic research, which aimed at renewing the deck of cards. It is the result of a typographic creation and combination of figures and letters. The logo gave birth to the game. The choice of the colors and their effect on the material was dealt with using the same care. This project plays with the established codes in order to create a new object which is graphical and conceptual and which fits into a contemporary framework.

Design/ Lajos Major

_B_E_U_U_

This is a "Letter-Fetish" project in which we used Fraktur and Grotesque letters made of paper. The best way to learn the alphabet is by aggressive osmosis. This project was created in cooperation with Dorottya Vékony.

Design/ Lajos Major

_A_U_S_T_

We created a letter juggling theater, where the actor, like a seal, balances letters on the tip of his or her nose. Stories are told through the composition of different words using the characters. This project was created in cooperation with Dorottya Vékony.

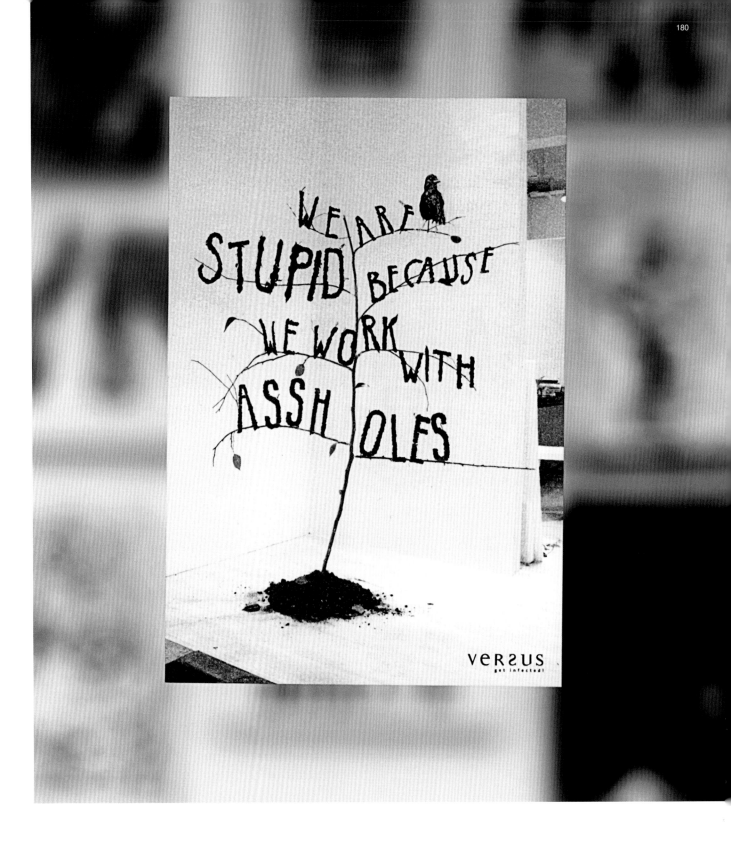

Design Agency/ Thinking*Room
Design/ Thinking*Room
Illustration/ Steven Dian Maryko
Client/ Versus Magazine
Photography/ Putra Agung

WE ARE STUPID

On one occasion, *Versus Magazine* invited illustrators and designers to submit a piece of artwork for their limited edition designer postcard series. Our brief came just before the deadline. This was quite a spontaneous quote that passes through many people's minds; it's an accumulation of experiences in the service industry that taught us many valuable lessons about life and people. Since there is no such thing as a bad client, the person to blame for a bad project is the designer who undertakes the wrong project.

EAT BAG

The project was given to us by Cork & Screw, a wine lounge located on South Jakarta. We were already working with them to develop their identity, so we had a good idea of their spirit and its expression in visual form. For the bag design, we hid three characters within a composition of punctuation marks. The overall type composition formed an abstracted image shape. The three characters can be read as a word, as well. This bag is all about a subtle, but visible, well-embedded message.

Design Agency/ Thinking*Room
Design/ Thinking*Room
Client/ Cork & Screw
Photography/ Putra Agung

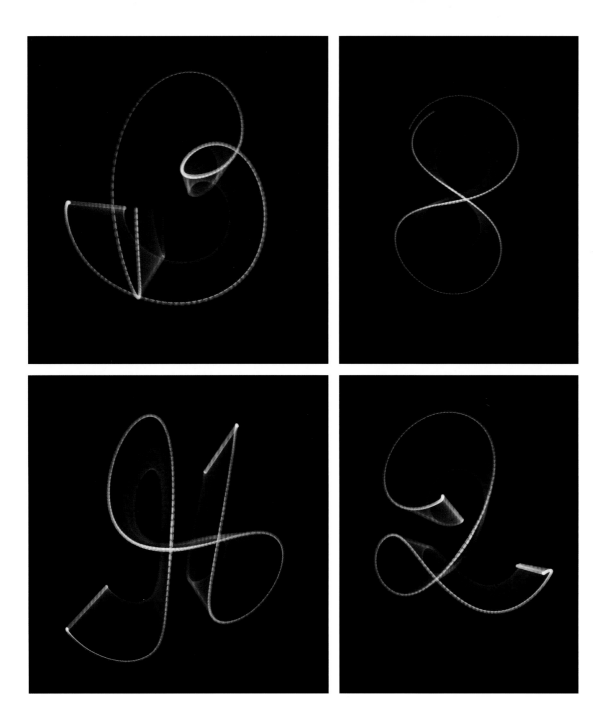

Design/ LoSiento

LED A PORTER

Led a Porter is a firm that manufactures LEDs and also takes over lighting projects. The alphabet for this project has been designed using only the light provided by LEDs. With a color bar and a long photographic exposure, the whole alphabet was created. The lettering was used to illustrate the brand's catalogue and stationery.

Design/ Tim Fishlock

ALPHABET RELIEF

This alphabet was designed as a limited edition print.

Design/ David Torrents
Client/ Adifad

DELTA AWARDS 09

The project consisted of a visual identity, communication campaign and environmental design. Delta Awards is an important competition for industrial designers to promote the best products distributed in Spain.

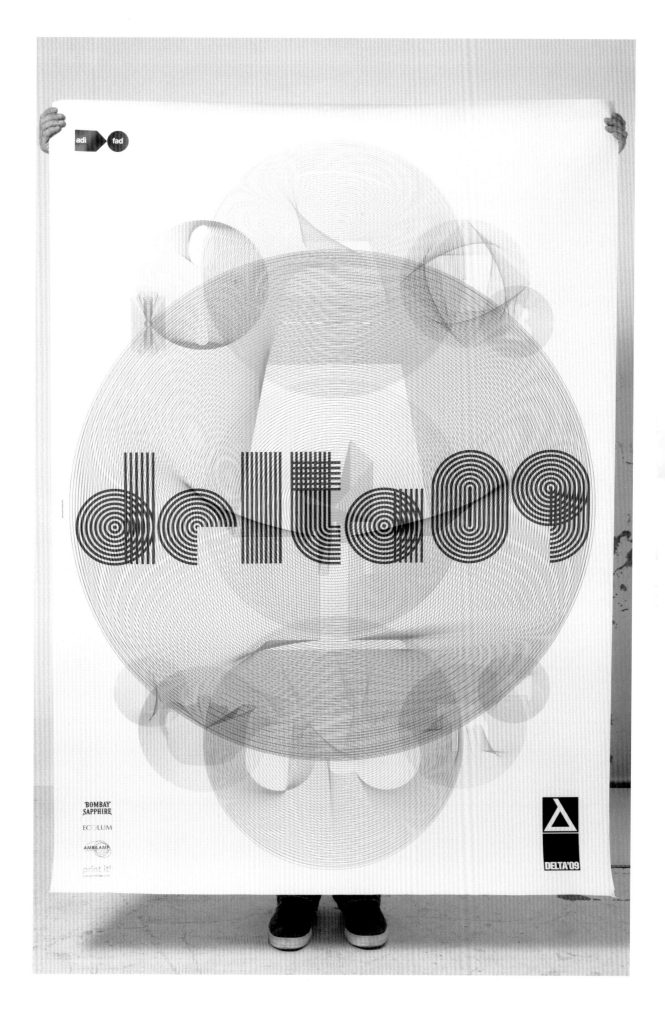

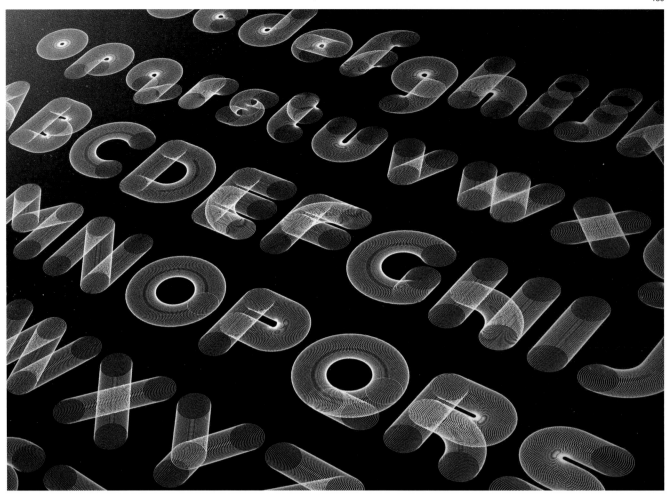

Design/ Paul Hollingworth

SLINKYTYPE

A simple, yet visually compelling type experiment using repetitive linear shapes to form letters. A tribute to the classic slinky.

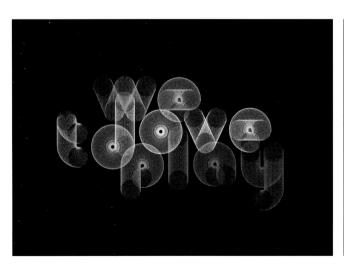

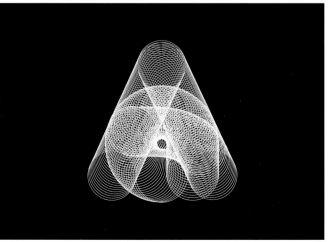

Design Agency/ I LIKE BIRDS contemporary design &
experimental lab
Design/ I LIKE BIRDS
Illustration/ I LIKE BIRDS
Client/ THE BEARDSHOP

HI

Silkscreen print for a shopping bag. A contribution to
interact with your city and give a warm welcome to
everyone on the street. We also designed some pins
which come along with the bag and are attached
to its interior, instead of a sewn label.

Design Agency/ I LIKE BIRDS contemporary design & experimental lab
Design/ I LIKE BIRDS
Illustration/ I LIKE BIRDS

I LIKE

A self promotional artwork and experimental typeface made of different materials. The concept was to combine the shapes of simple, non-colored objects to create interesting spacial tensions and variations.

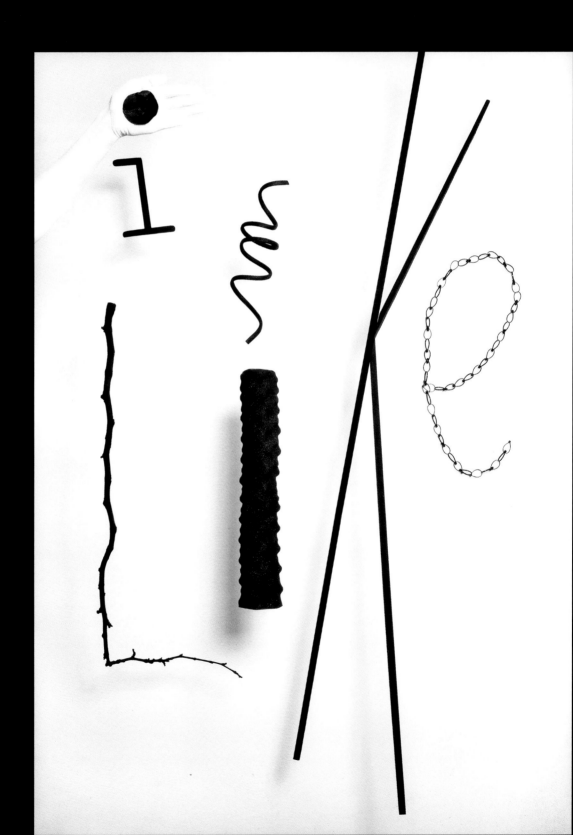

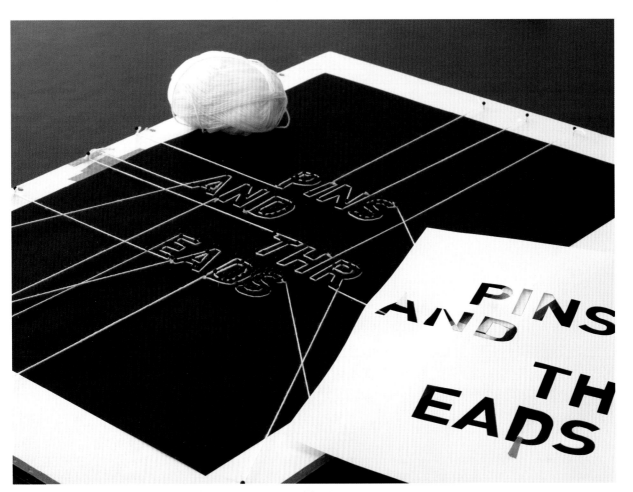

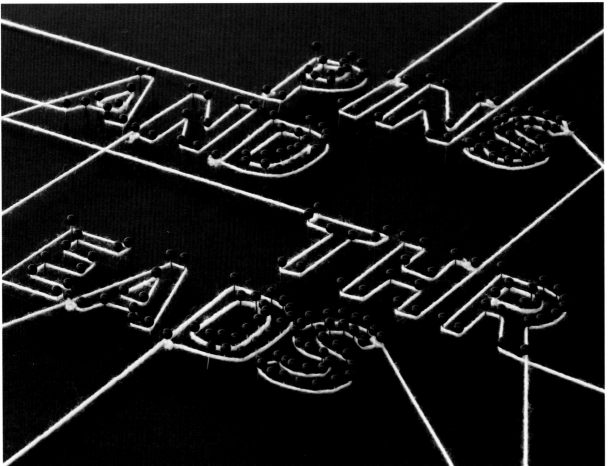

01   THE BURNING ROOM
02   PINS AND THREADS
03   ARTIFICIAL
04   MINOR PROBLEMS
05   NEAT
06   MOST RULES ARE STUPID
07   INSERT DISC
08   A TERRIFIC TRANSITION
09   ATTACK OF THE ARCHITECTS
10   SWEEPING FLOORS
11   LIKE A HUNT
12   PATHOS

Design/ Kasper Pyndt
Client/ re-public

PINS AND THREADS

During an internship with re-public in Copenhagen I was asked to produce some graphic work with thread as my main tool. I attached pins to a board and strung out white thread between them to form the words "pins and threads" (I know, kind of an obvious title). Then I was asked to make the piece into a poster, and finally I had to make the poster into a CD cover. The main idea of this exercise was to learn to adjust to a new problem and a new medium, and to see things in a different context.

Design/ Akatre

LIGHT THE FIRE

Invitation for a private party.

FRACTURE

The aim of this project was to create a work of graphic design that was 3-dimensional. The idea of typography as installation eventually led to the development of a typeface that, through its dimensionality, became unreadable from certain angles. Aimed towards other graphic designers, the project served to challenge the objective of typography.

The resulting typeface, "Disjointed," was constructed by breaking apart the anatomy of letterforms, pushing each part into a different plane, thereby disconnecting the structure through depth. The poster for the typeface reads, "put things into perspective" and touches on the different perspectives of what the role of type should be. From different angles, the type is both legible and illegible, touching on the core of the debate of the function of type.

Design Agency/ Studio mw
Design/ Studio mw
Illustration/ Studio mw
Client/ Self Initiated Work

MANNEQUINS

Mannequins is a series of portraits and typographies. It tries to question and define the idea of physical and graphical perfection in our modern society, and tends to suggest a new vision of modeling where portraits and typography use the modern codes of beauty in order to bend and break them. The project was created in order to interfere with the accepted graphic codes of advertisements. The spectator discovers each illustration and is surrounded by an aesthetically tortured world. The main element is a typographic blend of the codes of masculine and feminine modeling. The project reshapes the physical aspects of the models by confronting them; the typography overshadows the humanity, and communication takes precedence.

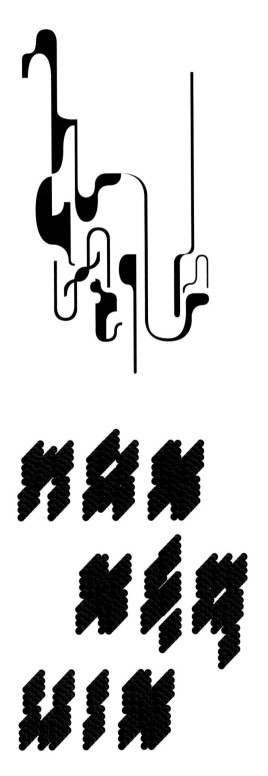

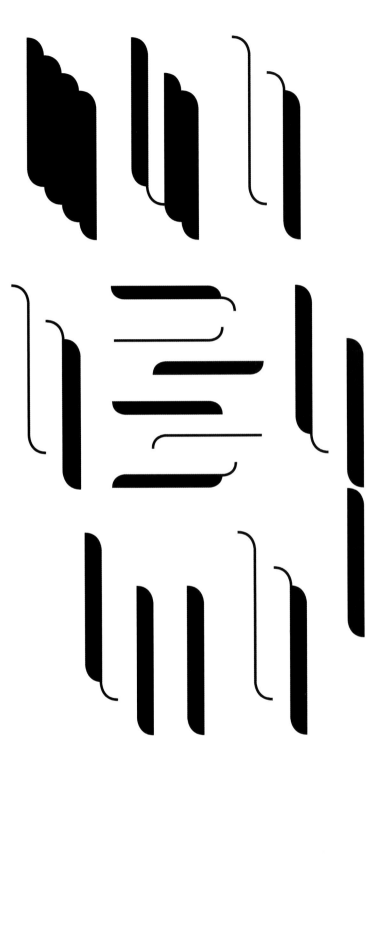

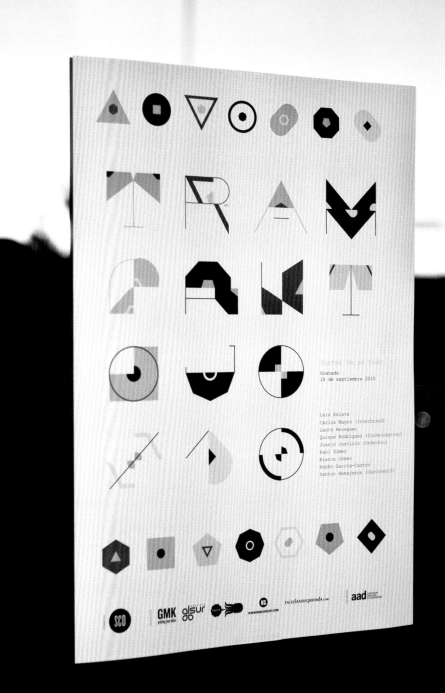

Design/ Romualdo Faura
Client/ Soy Cultura del Diseño
Photography/ Alfonso Acedo

TRAMPANTOJO

Trampantojo is a design event in Granada, Spain. It is organized by Soy Cultura del Diseño, an association of graphic designers. The identity of this year was based on two concepts: the isolation of one part of the design, and the unification of the whole. Every design project is composed of parts: clients, ideas, sketches, fonts, colors, etc...

Speakers talked about the processes in their projects of design and illustration. Project identity is constructed from basic shapes that represent the whole, and the shapes are divided into parts in order to make letters and symbols. These letters were used to build the names of the speakers and signage for the event.

Design/ Alex Camacho
Client/ Self Initiated Work

MODULAR TYPOGRAPHY

Alex designed this Modular Typography from the division of a
circle and a triangle. Inspired by the simplicity and geometry
of the Bauhaus.

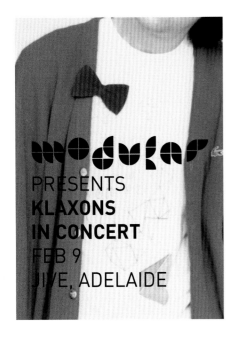

Design/ Linna Xu

MODULAR

The challenge of this project was to create a corporate identity system for an independent Australian record production company called Modular (People). Modular means to be composed of repeating units that can shift and be reorganized, and this was a core idea that was reiterated in the visual branding. The modular form of a quarter circle was derived from breaking a record into four pieces. This shape was then used to compose all of the other elements within the identity system. The presence of a human quality and interactivity were also central to the brand. For example, each employee has photos of themselves interacting with the typeface that they can stick on letterheads as personalized signatures, and the website shows hands coming in to rearrange the quarter-circle pieces to form different words for each section. All of these elements result in a modular system that allows flexibility to generate multiple forms that still consistently represent the company.

Design Agency/ Tiana Vasiljev
Design/ Tiana Vasiljev
Client/ Valentine Associates
Photography/ Tiana Vasiljev

EIGHTEEN PERCENT
TYPEFACE & BRANDING

Eighteen Percent is the photographic division of
Valentine Associates, a Sydney-based graphic
design studio. The logo was created from a
typeface designed exclusively for Eighteen Percent.
A collection of negatives that had recently been
processed was the inspiration behind the typeface,
and the final logo and alphabet represent qualities
evident in both digital and analog photography.
The typeface and brand extension was carried
throughout all stationery and helped in creating a
simple, fun and informative identity.

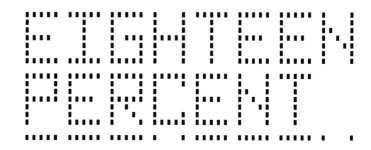

Design Agency/ I LIKE BIRDS contemporary design & experimental lab
Design/ I LIKE BIRDS
Illustration/ I LIKE BIRDS
Photography/ I LIKE BIRDS

HAPPY PEPPY

This experimental typeface was our contribution to a typographic calendar. The main idea was to develop a font linked to a positive experience and a happy emotion. We built the letters by using ribbon, which is associated with unwrapping presents. After the font was finished, we decided to design a poster to show the typeface in its execution — ending up with the happy fox and the happy dog. The poster is printed offset on a "jogging pants-look-alike" paper and is available at www.thebeardshop.de.

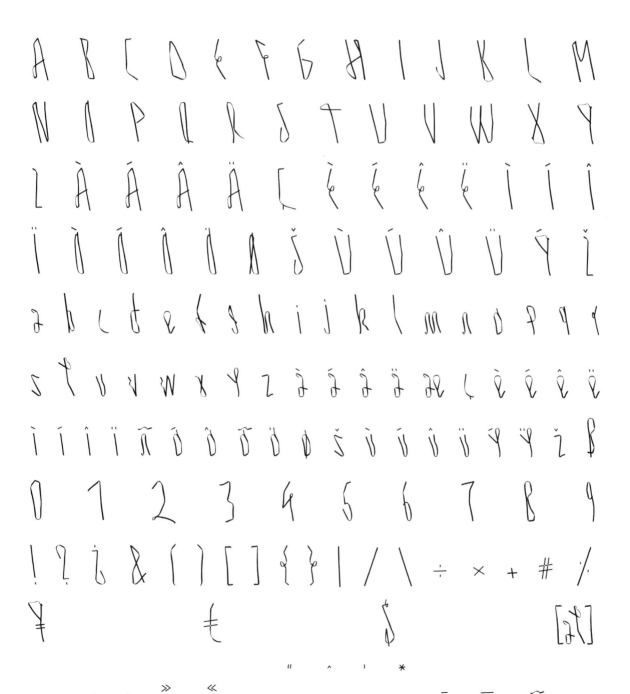

Design Agency/ Type Fabric | Atelier für Gestaltung
Design/ Type Fabric ©
Client/ Openair Mutterschiff

OPENAIR MUTTERSCHIFF

The open air festival Mutterschiff takes place on the site of a
construction company with stacked tools, wood, and other
materials. The festival focuses on this idea of building and
creation, which is why the poster features type made out of
old letterpress wood letters. The typography is also built up like
the brick walls of a building. The words on the poster are put
together letter by letter, as if by a construction worker on a
construction site. This references the historical roots of careful
typeface composition in our profession as typesetters.

Design Agency/ PinkLab
Design/ PinkLab

"PLASTIC BAG" FONT TYPE

A new and original font type is designed in this project. As the environmental problems caused by the overuse of plastic bags are serious, a set of "Plastic Bag" letters was designed to increase awareness of this problem.

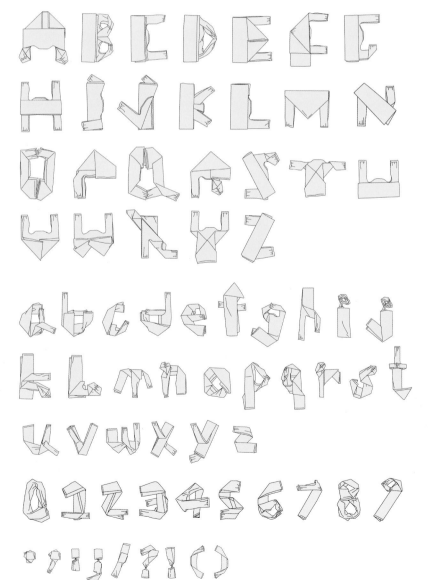

Design/ Hoyt Haffelder

CUBE YOUR LIFE

Cube Your Life is a project inspired by the Rubik's
cube. Hoyt Haffelder started by creating a typeface
based on a three-quarter view of a cube. Then he
designed a set of postal stamps. The application also
extended into a T-shirt. To facilitate the utility of the
typeface he put together actual cubes representing
the two-dimensional type. The goal of the project
was to bring type into a new dimension by giving it
greater depth.

Design/ Allan Sommerville

CONDENSED LANGUAGE

Allan's MA (at the London College of Communication) focused on typographic ligatures. Specifically, his interest was how these special characters could be used in today's digital environment where language is often abbreviated and condensed.

E-mail and text messaging have transformed the way in which we send messages but other technologies such as text recognition software suggest that the handwritten letter may become a thing of the past. Inspiration for the project came from a variety of sources — from Herbert Bayer and Jan Tschichold's modernist alphabets of the 1920s through to more recent experiments by Philipp Stamm and Pierre Di Sciullo. Allan used an existing typeface, "TheSans" by Luc(as) de Groot, to create new ligatured characters which could be used alongside different spelling proposals, phonetic alphabets or shorthand systems.

Design Agency/ 26+
Design/ Jakob Runge

FRACMETRICA BLACK TYPEFACE

This typeface combines geometric typography with black letter and fashionable Didones with an isometric grid underneath. The font is equipped with some OpenType features and is free for non-commercial use.

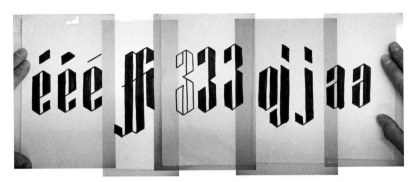

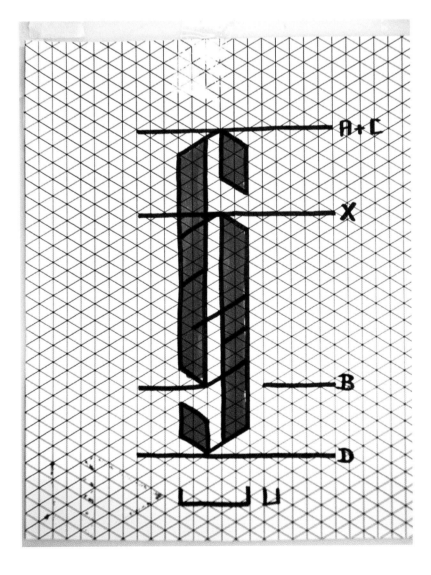

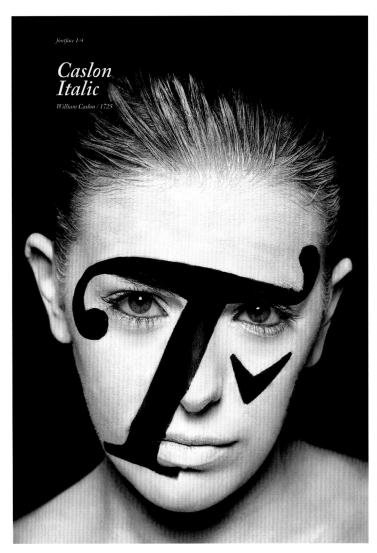

fontface 1/4

Caslon
Italic

William Caslon / 1725

fontface 2/4

Clarendon
Bold

William Thorowgood / 1845

Design/ Atipo
Photography/ Atipo

FONTFACE

Our idea was to combine real works with self-initiated projects and Fontface is one of them. We really like typography; we think it is the foundation of design and it has great communication power. We wanted to make typographic posters, even though we knew there are not many good design projects in this field. We were aware that it would be necessary to look for another point of view. We came up with our idea upon seeing the work of photographer Erwin Olaf — in particular, the "Paradise porting" portrait series. We thought that make-up could be used as a typographic element and a human face could be the background for a typographic series.

We have chosen four typographies from four outstanding type designers and we tried to combine the expression of gesture and text, as well as make a brief journey through typographic history. The trajectory goes from a traditional Roman letter style like Caslon to a slab serif like Clarendon, to a grotesque type like Helvetica, to didone, like Carousel. We chose the characters that epitomize the main features of each typeface, and most importantly, they operated as a mask on the model's face.

We looked for an almost painterly effect, where the imperfections add expressiveness to the proposal. The characters were drawn directly without any technical assistance, only referring to a preliminary sketch on the laptop screen. The entire project, from work, concept, and makeup, to photography and video, was completed by members of the studio.

fontface 3/4

Helvetica
Bold

Max Miedinger / 1956

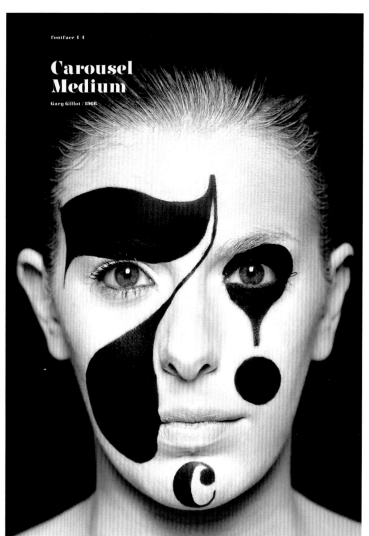

fontface 4/4

Carousel
Medium

Gary Gillot / 1966

PLAY

"Play" was my final graduation project for the Academy of Fine Arts Maastricht in the Netherlands. Working with real things in a three-dimensional space allows me to minimize the actual distance between myself and the object. This happens without any computer support. In my opinion, design feels more realistic and alive this way; it can be slightly inaccurate, but in a good way. This adds a sense of ease to my work. Handmade things show imperfections; this happens accidentally or as a result of experimentation. It is simply the side effect of having fun and playing around. Through hand-produced projects, the designer becomes involved with the image and becomes a vivid part of it. I believe design is all about fun. Play is the beginning of every invention, and it's how we learn. Play helps children learn to be adults by exploring the world, and it's how we feel alive. It's so easy — just play!

Design Agency/ Me Studio
Design/ Martin Pyper

SUIKERDEPÔT IDENTITY

"Het Suikerdepôt" is a small film-production company housed in an old sugar
factory bearing the same name. This was the starting point for the typeface
which is built entirely from sugar cubes placed on a small piece of pink
newsprint. The font was used to create different words on all printed matter
and the website, etc. Me Studio has also made several posters and flyers for
exhibitions and other events using "sugar cube" illustrations.

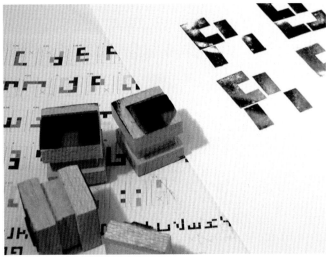

Design/ Nello Russo
Photography/ Nello Russo

PEECSO FONT

Peecso is an experimental design for a pixel-geometric font envisioned as a back and forth communication. Each letter is composed of the same 6 pairs of graphic elements which build a basic unit (the square), as well as multiples of this unit (rectangles) in groups of 2 or 4.

The creative process involved the production of 6 double-faced rubber stamps which were used as an analogy prototype for the font set.

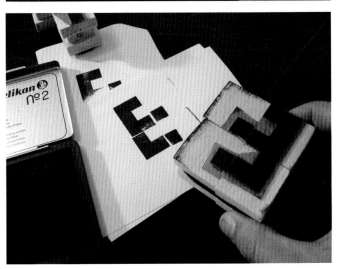

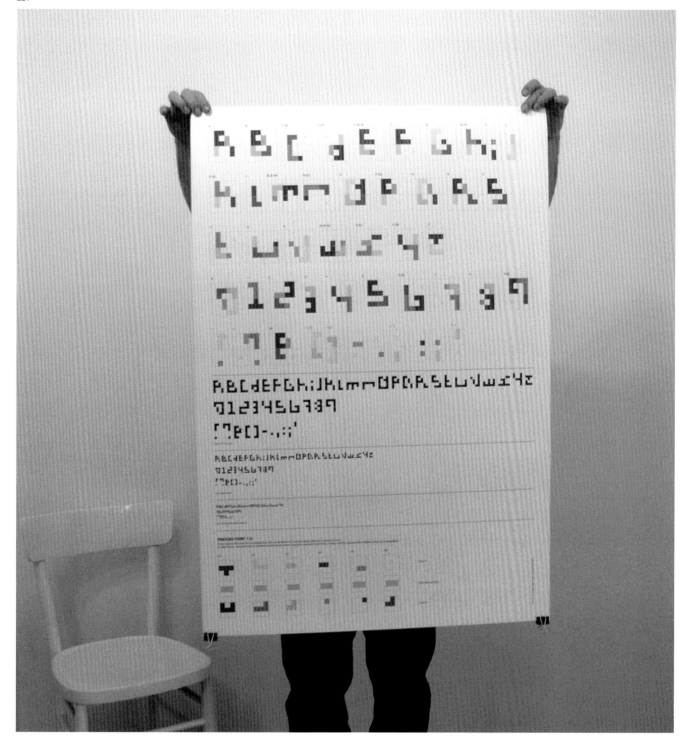

C U R V E S T I T C H   T Y P O G R A P H Y

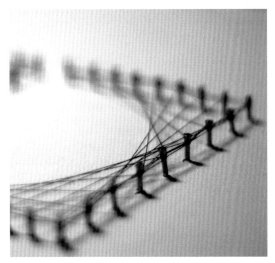

Design/ Thom Isom
Client/ Self Initiated Work
Photography/ Thom Isom

LUDD–CURVESTITCH TYPOGRAPHY

Curve-stitch typography entitled "Ludd" which was created in April 2010. The typeface has been created in both digital and handcrafted formats with each letter nailed and threaded through 26 separate A4 boards. The entire process was developed through the technique of curve stitch alone.

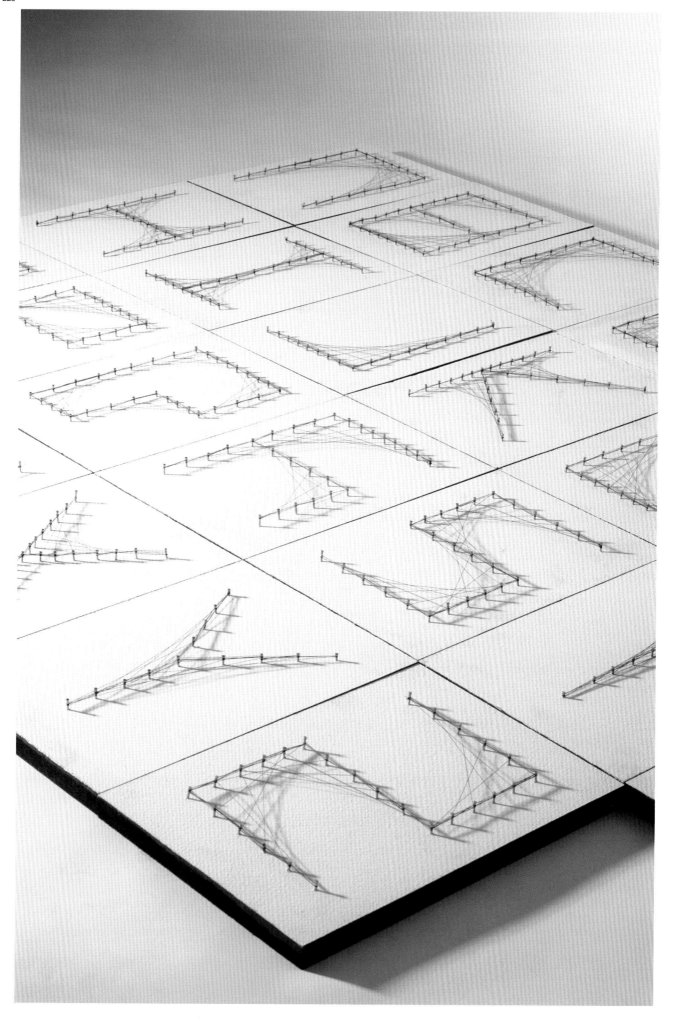

Design/ Patrycja Zywert
Photography/ Self Initiated Work

HOW MUCH DOES YOUR BUILDING WEIGH, MR. FOSTER?

This project is a typographic installation and a poster advertising the film about British architect Norman Foster titled "How Much Does Your Building Weigh, Mr. Foster?" The idea is to express the striking feel of Foster's architecture by creating large geometric forms for the letters F, O, S, T, E and R.

For one of my previous projects I designed an exhibition celebrating the life of Norman Foster. He created, and still creates, the world's landmark office buildings. The recent release of a film about Foster was one of the inspirations for me to create another piece of graphic work based on architecture and geometry. I decided to focus on the shapes often seen in Foster's designs — triangles and squares. Continuing my research about the relationship between typography and architecture, I set out on the task of creating an architectural typography installation promoting the film. The focus is on a 3D typeface inspired by Foster's buildings and the poster is designed around that. Apart from advertising the film, the installation aspires to celebrate the life of Foster by becoming his architectural signature. The typography could be displayed in all the cities which have buildings designed by this architect.

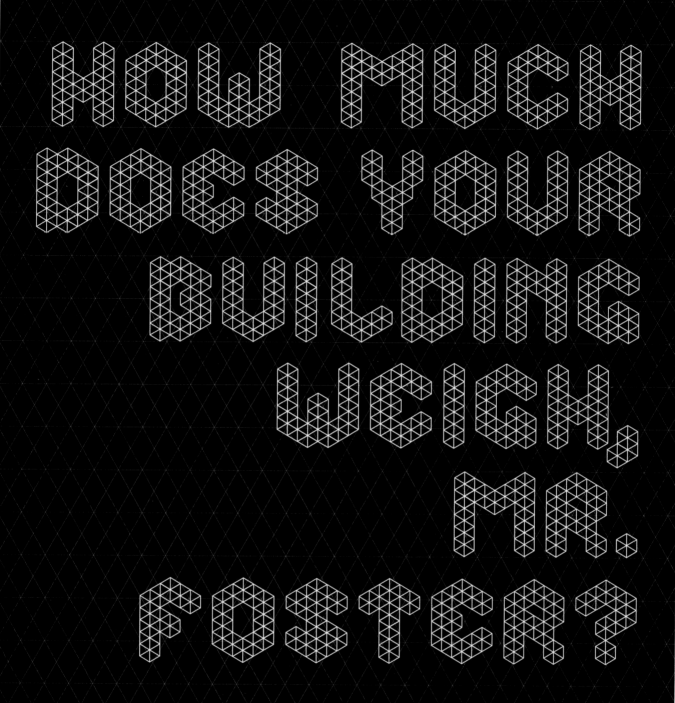

HOW MUCH DOES YOUR BUILDING WEIGH, MR. FOSTER?

DIRECTED BY **NORBERTO LOPEZ AMADO & CARLOS CARCAS** PRODUCER **ELENA OCHOA** EXECUTIVE PRODUCER **ANTONIO SANZ** WRITTEN AND NARRATED BY **DEYAN SUDJIC** DIRECTOR OF PHOTOGRAPHY **VALENTIN ALVAREZ**
MUSIC BY **JOAN VALENT** FILM EDITOR **PACO COZAR** LINE PRODUCER **PALOMA LOPEZ VAZQUES** AN **ART COMISSIONERS** PRODUCTION IN ASSOCIATION WITH **AIETE ARIANE FILMS**
MORE INFORMATION AND PRESS MATERIALS AT WWW.ARTCOMISSIONERS.COM

Design/ Thom Bradley, Rich Stangroom
Client/ Kingston University

KNIGHTS PARK IDENTITY

The winning pitch for re-brand of the Knights Park campus identity. The identity is a modular system based on the playful creativity and strong structural forms of the campus itself. The identity grew from a typeface into a way-finding system, full stationery design and website animation.

Design/ Thom Bradley

CRADLE TO CRADLE

A print campaign designed to promote a series of lectures on the cradle to cradle design framework. The 360 degree poster emulates the cradle to cradle theory with a continuous print taking over the space in which it is placed.

SKATE

This was a project commissioned by skate magazine Uno Mag. LoSiento was asked to illustrate the letter E from the word SKATE. All the letters are composed using a skater's silhouette making a particular skate maneuver.

"E" Fakie tailslide varial flip out

AD: Losiento Studio / Ph: Ferran Izquierdo

Design Agency/ Gluekit
Design/ Gluekit
Client/ RBM: A Journal of Rare Books, Manuscripts, and Cultural Heritage

DIVERSITY

Typographic cover for RBM: A Journal of Rare Books, Manuscripts, and Cultural Heritage. The idea behind the design was to use hands of various shades combining and re-combining simple geometric shapes to create the letter-forms in the word "DIVERSITY" — a simple way to illuminate the theme of the magazine special issue.

Design/ Lara Lozano

BUIT (VACUUM)

Alphabet creation from the study of the external shape
of the character. Each character has been created
with sheets covering the external shape, allowing the
characters to be formed by the negative space left in
the middle of each draping.

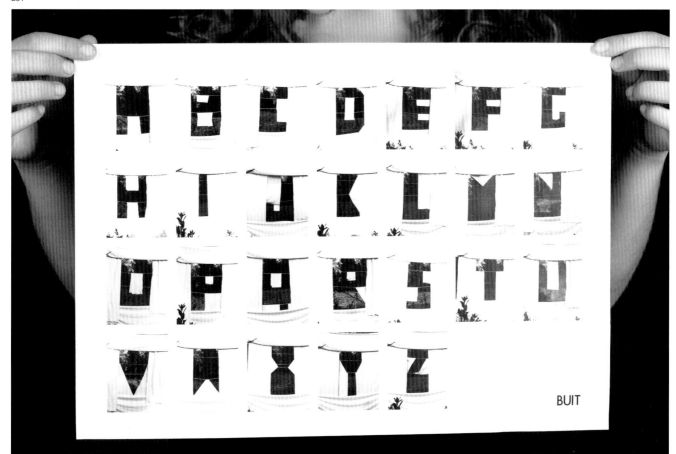

BUIT

BUIT:

AQUESTA TIPOGRAFIA NO VOL SER UNA
TIPOGRAFIA DE TEXT, ÉS TOTALMENT EXPERI-
MENTAL. CADA UNA DE LES LLETRES ÉS UNA
PETITA INTERVENCIÓ EN L'ESPAI I UN ESTUDI
DE LA FORMA DE LES LLETRES A PARTIR DE LA
CONTRAFORMA. EN AQUESTA TIPOGRAFIA,
LA LLETRA APAREIX DEL BUIT QUE DEIXEN LES
SEVES CONTRAFORMES.

PROCÉS DE LA
TIPOGRAFIA
BUIT

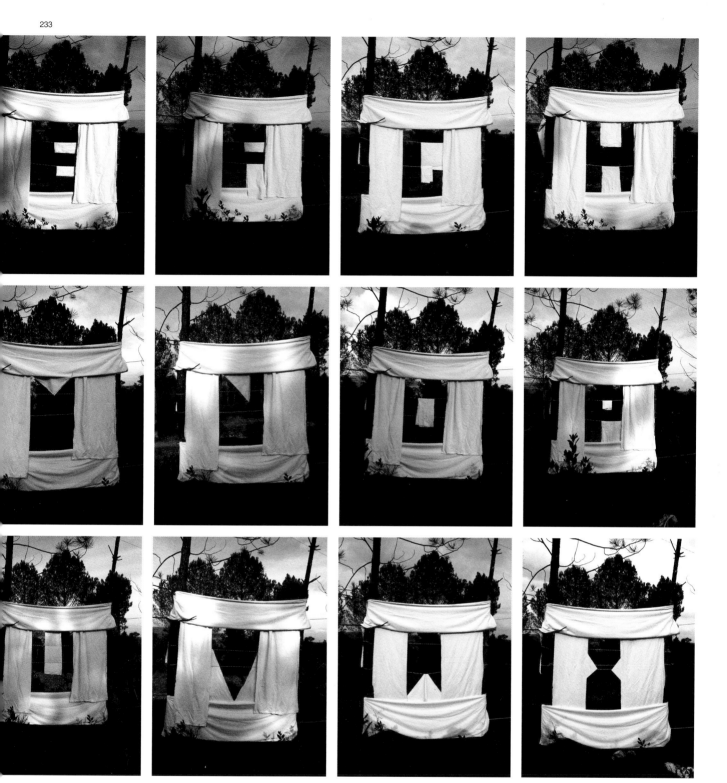

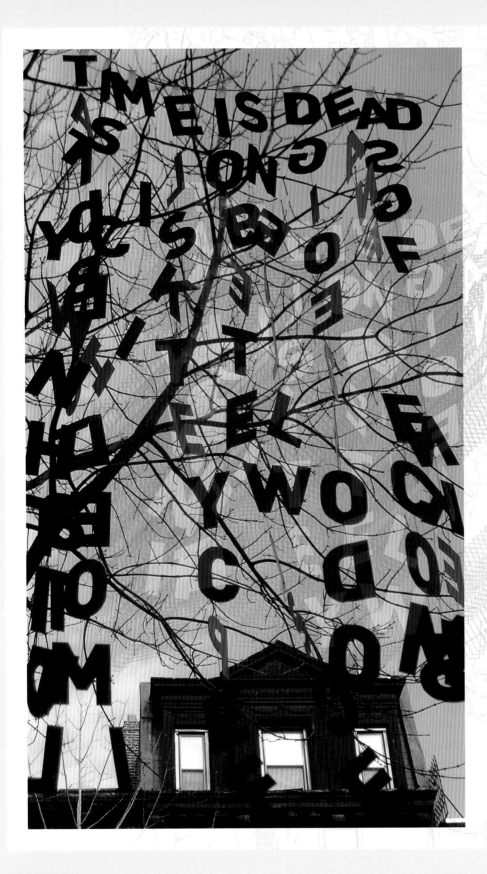

Design/ John Lepak
Photography/ John Lepak

TIME/VISIBLE/DEAD/INVISIBLE

The two posters were designed as part of a Senior Project class at Pratt Institute. The assignment was to take two otherwise unrelated quotes and to create a pair of related posters. John chose to explore William Faulkner's *The Sound and the Fury*, and Oscar Wilde's *The Picture of Dorian Grey*. John took from both quotes a sense of a physical, tangible world, and so decided to step away from the computer and use his hands. This resulted in a set of hand-cut letters submitted to the context of their respective quote. For the Faulkner poster he strung the letters up as a sort of typographic mobile and subjected them to the elements. For the Wilde, he used the negatives of the letters to reflect the quote.

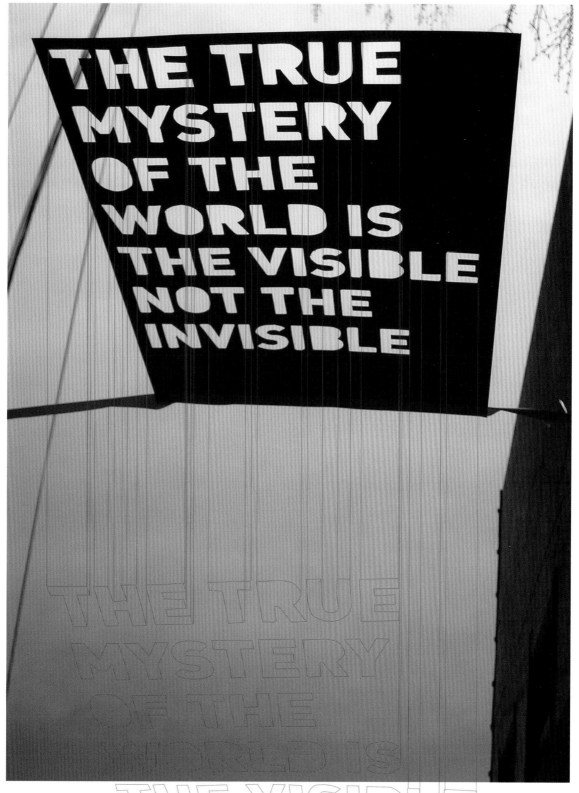

Design/ Staynice
Client/ Self Initiated Work

HOUSE BECOMES HOTEL

Experimental artwork in an abandoned house.

Design Agency/ Staynice
Design/ Staynice
Client/ Breda Barst Festival

BREDA BARST

Hand painted graphic on wood.

Design Agency/ Staynice
Design/ Staynice
Client/ Playgrounds Audiovisual Festival

PLAYGROUNDS

Hand painted typographic design for Playgrounds
Audiovisual Arts Festival 2009.

Design/ Kasper Pyndt, Jeppe Drensholt

TWIN PEAKS STENCILS

Kasper's class at Krabbesholm (a graphic design foundation) was asked to decorate a room for a party with "Twin Peaks" as the theme. The students were divided into small groups and each group made a large scale stencil out of a quote from "Twin Peaks," to be painted on the floors and walls. Jeppe Drensholt and Kasper Pyndt chose the quote "The only thing Columbus discovered was that he was lost," which kind of makes sense when one sees the puzzle of words on the floor. The party was a great success.

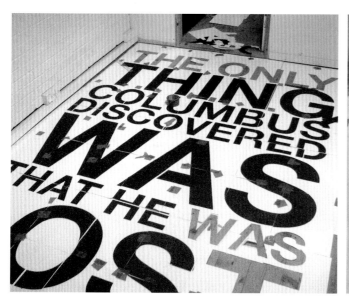

Design/ Sergio Alves
Client/ Terra na Boca

YOU GO

This poster was created for a Contemporary Dance event by Hajime Fujita where rolls of toilet paper were used during the performance, which inspired the idea of creating the type for the poster solely from rolls of toilet paper. The title of the performance, "You Go Where You Should Go," is quite long. I decided to create the poster in quite large dimensions and incorporate the artist himself into the typographic composition.

The floor of a large room in an art gallery was covered in a large (16 feet x 10 feet) black piece of material spread over the floor. Small pieces of information were still missing. I considered the idea of adding additional information digitally later, but preferred to work without digital manipulation. We only had the use of the gallery for one day and I needed a solution for how to add the additional information. I visited the supermarket to see what I could find and came across some packs of cotton which are used for removing make-up. These "pads" were used to form the letters for the information which had been missing. Last of all, the artist's form was integrated into the phrase as he moved in various positions on the material, until I finally discovered the ideal position for him within the piece. The only items added digitally were the logos.

TERRA NA BOCA
YOU GO.
7-8 DEZ.
WHERE.
22H
ESTÚDIO LATINO
YOU SHOULD GO.
ESTRUTURA FINANCIADA POR:
M|C Ministério da Cultura
dgARTES Direcção-Geral das Artes
M/12 WWW.TERRANABOCA.COM

Akatre
France

Akatre is a graphic design studio based in Paris. The studio was created by Valentin Abad, Julien Dhivert and Sébastien Riveron. Their work includes photography, global design, signs, posters, artistic installations, and new media (videos, animation, DVD creation, websites, etc.).

Alex Camacho
Spain

Through studying graphic design at Elisava University and working in diverse design studios across Barcelona, Alex was finally able to discover his true passion in life: typography. Upon making this realization, he decided to pack his bags and move to New York City to strengthen his calligraphy skills at Cooper Union for the Advancement of Science and Art. Later, Alex was accepted to the Communication Design masters program at Central Saint Martins in London. He is currently in his first year and is studying Typography and Language and also working as a freelancer.

Allan Sommerville
UK

Allan Sommerville is the owner of Blokgraphic, a London design studio specialising in print and publishing. He studied illustration at Edinburgh Art School and more recently completed an MA in graphic design at the London College of Communication which has brought a new creative perspective to his commercial projects.

Amandine Alessandra
UK

Amandine Alessandra is a French graphic designer based in London. She studied Fine Arts at the Université de Provence in France and later Graphic Design at the London College of Communication in the UK. Her current research looks at augmenting a message's signal through installations and photography, while drawing relationships between a place, a statement and hand-made typography devised for a specific context.

Andrew Effendy
Indonesia

Andrew Effendy is of Chinese descent but was born in Indonesia. He graduated from the California State University Long Beach graphic design program in 2009. He currently lives and works as a graphic designer in Los Angeles. He likes noodles and meatballs.

Anton Gridz
Kazakhstan

Anton Gridz is 24 years old. He was born in Kazakhstan in a small enclosed military town. After the collapse of the USSR he lived and studied in Vinnitsa, Ukraine. Now he is living and work in Kiev. He likes good music, books, sports, and travel.

Atipo
Spain

Atipo is a small multidisciplinary studio that was founded in early 2010 by Raúl García del Pomar and Ismael González and based in Gijón (Spain). After several years working for others in branding consultancy, web design and graphic design, they thought it was time to launch a personal project that allowed them to develop the work from a personal point of view. Their background in Fine Arts allows them to combine different disciplines (typography, photography, painting, illustration and video) and produce each work through experimentation.

Autobahn
the Netherlands

Autobahn is an internationally distinguished graphic design studio that creates unique design solutions and products out of love for the profession. This is reflected in strong typography and a keen eye for form and content. Each product is unique in its approach, concept and execution but there is always one constant factor: atypical Autobahn design which often results in the use of striking materials. No matter what kind of project, Autobahn accepts the challenge on every level, whether it's a strategic proposal, a complete campaign or experimentation with new designs!

Borja Martínez
Spain

Borja Martínez founded his own studio LoSiento in 2005, which gathers a team of 5 professionals and works in the fields of corporate identity, packaging, editorial, and in self-initiated projects as well. Their philosophy is based on taking over the whole concept of each identity project. In 2010, LoSiento was given a grant by the FAD (Fomento de las Artes Decorativas) and received the Grand Laus award. The main feature of LoSiento is an organic and physical approach to solutions, resulting in a field where graphic and industrial design have dialogue, in a constant search for an alliance with artisan processes.

Brian Banton
Canada

Brian is a freelance graphic designer and part-time faculty member of the Department of Design at York University. He holds a Master of Design from York University and Bachelor of Design from the Ontario College of Art and Design in Toronto, Canada.

Casper Chan Ka Lok
UK

Graphic designer, illustrator and stylist currently based in London. He graduated from The Hong Kong Polytechnic University, School of Design in 2006 with a major in visual communication design. His portfolio diversely synthesizes typography, illustration and fashion styling. In 2009, he was awarded the British council 60th anniversary scholarship for an MA in Graphic Design from the London College of Communication. In 2011, he formed Studio 247 with Monkey Leung in order to pursue their collaborative graphic design vision.

Corriette Schoenaerts
the Netherlands

Corriette Schoenaerts works in the fields of autonomous, fashion and commercial photography and refuses to draw any finite distinctions between these fields. According to her a recognizable style is "a cheap trick that fails to bring pleasure to yourself, your work or the public." Schoenaerts usually works in a series, creating parallel worlds that seem strangely real. She doesn't like revealing her ideas in a photo although she believes a photo shouldn't be a puzzle either. "Photography is often obvious enough."

David Torrents
Spain

David Torrents received a degree from Gerrit Rietveld Academie in Amsterdam and from the Faculty of Fine Arts at the University of Barcelona. He also studied at Elisava School for Design in Barcelona. He has worked in Amsterdam, Budapest, and in various studios and agencies in Barcelona.

David has been running a multidisciplinary design studio based in Barcelona since 2002. He designs books, posters, webpages, graphic identities, environmental design and motion, among other projects.

Ebon Heath
Germany

Ebon Heath splits his time between Brooklyn and Berlin. He received his BFA in Graphic Design from the Rhode Island School of Design in 1994. He founded "stereotype" the same year, a design studio focused on music packaging, magazine layout design, and fashion advertising. He co-founded Cell Out in 2003, a consultancy that develops issue-based media strategies for non-profits, NGO's and brands. He has exhibited internationally with his stereotype mobiles, installations, jewelry, and performance art bringing new life to typography. He is a visiting professor of Graphic Design at Lehman College in the Bronx (USA) and an Art Director for the Mindpirates Berlin (DE).

Elle Jeong Eun Kim
US

Elle Jeong Eun Kim is a graphic designer and a maker currently living in Brooklyn, NY. She graduated from Rhode Island School of Design with a BFA in graphic design and moved to NYC to work as a graphic designer in publishing, advertising and the fashion industry. After 5 years of working in NYC, she decided to pursue a master degree from Cranbrook Academy of Art in MI studying under Elliott Earls in the 2D Design department. Her biggest passion is in free form lettering and typography. Lately she's been working with typography in space creating an experience for viewers to engage with and have an emotional response to.

Erxu Chen
China

Graduated from the school of Design in the Central Academy of Fine Arts in 2009 and studied at studio 11.

Has been the project partner of the Digital Media Institute of Jiangnan University.

Co-founded the digital media studio Between Design.

Ethan Park
UK

Ethan was born in Korea. He received his MA in Communication Design from Kingston University, London.

Ethan is interested in the role of typography within communication and works across a range of media. He takes everyday objects such as food, clothing, and natural forms as a starting point for experimental typography through which objects appear in unexpected locations, where the division between type and image is blurred.

Farina Kuklinski
Germany

Farina Kuklinski is a graphic designer currently living and working in Berlin. She grew up in a small town in Germany located right next to the Dutch-Belgian border. Farina has always had a great affinity for those two countries. One of her main reasons for becoming a graphic designer was the wholehearted desire to communicate her thoughts and ideas to society and gain the expertise that would allow her to get lost in her own design ideas and the brilliant ideas of other designers.

Ferdi Alıcı
Turkey

Ferdi Alıcı is currently a student in the Visual Communication Design Department at Istanbul Bilgi University. He is also the founder of Ouchhh Motion & Interactive / Art Direction Company. He has been featured in many national and international catalogues and exhibitions such as Offf Paris Catalogue, Off Motion Fest (his works were displayed on Krakow buildings in POLAND), and MTV Playground's Prize, etc. He currently lives in Istanbul.

Gluekit
US

Gluekit is the design and illustration studio of American designers Kathleen Sleboda and Christopher Sleboda. Founded in 2002, Gluekit creates images, design, typography, patterns, and products for clients around the world. Gluekit's work investigates two-and three-dimensional spatial relationships, popular design motifs, fragments, the flexibility of language and representation, the intersection of handmade and computer-generated imagery, and the communication of ideas through simple graphics. The design studio's illustrations have graced the covers and interiors of hundreds of magazines.

Happycentro
Italy

Happycentro consists of Roberto Solieri, Federico Galvani, Giulio Grigollo, Andrea Manzati and the photographer Federico Padovani. The design studio was set up in 1998 in Verona. They have worked for various clients, both local agencies and major international companies. Their approach to design is always the same: whether the project is designing a logo, an advertising page, or a wall, or directing a commercial, it's always an opportunity to deal with a new problem. The studio believes the formula for beauty is a mix of complexity, order, and dedication. Besides commissioned work, the designers spend much energy on research and experiments in the areas of visual art, typography, and illustration.

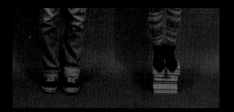

Hoyt Haffelder
US

Hoyt Haffelder received his Bachelor of Fine Arts in Communication Design from Texas State and returned for his Masters (MFA) in 2007. During pursuit of his MFA he has been employed as a designer in the office of University Marketing. Currently, he aligns internal departmental goals with overall university communication strategies, performs additional duties, and leads the charge in evolving the brand.

I LIKE BIRDS
Germany

I LIKE BIRDS is a small studio located in the Speicherstadt in the port of Hamburg composed of designers who turn design concepts into creations. They take great pleasure in experimenting with various mediums to develop customized and interesting solutions. Their activities focus on transforming numerous types of information into a visual language which conveys the content in a more fluid and effective manner.

They put a lot of time and effort into creating a wide range of print products, including posters, books, illustrations, corporate identities and other visual works for cultural and public purposes.

Iina Vuorivirta
Finland

Through her work, Iina Vuorivirta aims to express the belief that design can be smart, beautiful, and full of potential. She designs all messages, materials, and communication to support each other, in order to produce the strongest final result. She discovers problems revealed through everyday life, and then designs three-dimensional solutions which are imbued with meaning. She lives for the ups and downs of the design process and works with a particular consciousness of space and the relationships of objects to space.

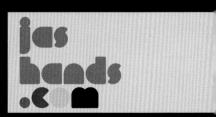

Jakob Runge
Germany

Jakob Runge is a German design student who specializes in type and graphic design. After receiving his Bachelor of Arts degree at the University of Applied Sciences in Würzburg, he began a Masters Degree program at the Muthesius

Jarrik Muller
The Netherlands

Jarrik Muller is an Amsterdam based design studio specialized in printed media, creative concepts, art direction, graphic design and typography. The work is strongly based on concepts, as form follows concept.

Jas Bhachu
UK

Primarily a print based graphic design studio that covers all areas of design. Jas Bhachu especially likes working with typography and experimenting with type to see how far he can push the boundaries of typography. In particular, he likes to break down

Jess Atkinson
Canada

Jess Atkinson is a Canadian designer currently dividing her time between Brooklyn, NY and Toronto, Canada. You'll often be able to find her sitting on a street curb counting pebbles, in the corner of a room, or sitting on a patio chair outside the laundromat. Any other time she'll be out with friends, eating an avocado sandwich or making plasticine artworks.

Johanna Hullár
Hungary

Johanna Hullár is a young graphic designer from Hungary. She has been studying Communication Design in HTW Berlin, Germany since 2009. She has had exhibition design jobs in Cetate / Calafat, Romania, and worked in a photography workshop in 2008.

John Lepak
US

John Lepak is a graphic designer from Hartford, Connecticut.

Jozef Ondrík
Slovakia

Jozef Ondrík was born in 1988 in Slovakia, where he studied at the School of Applied Arts. After that, he began studies at Tomas Bata University in Zlin (Czech Republic) in the department of Graphic Design and Typography. He is continuously looking for new possibilities, overlaps and functions within the fields of Design and Typography. His creativity is inspired by music, architecture, street art, travel, and his surroundings. He currently works as a freelancer. He runs small workshops and discussions on the theme of graphic design and typography in Slovakia.

Juan Camilo Rojas
US

Juan Camilo Rojas is a Colombian-born, Miami-Paris based graphic designer who graduated from the New World School of the Arts. His work is mainly based on typography and experimentation with typography as an art form. His work seeks to connect with viewers in order to communicate a certain message and to make them think, analyze, and build a link with the work.

Kasper Pyndt
Denmark

Kasper Pyndt is a 22-year-old graphic designer and illustrator from Copenhagen, Denmark. His work mainly focuses on illustration and typography. In the autumn of 2009 he lived and interned in Berlin. After that he returned to Copenhagen, where he worked for about 8 months with NR2154, a graphic design studio with print as its main focus. He currently is studying for a BA in Visual Communication at The Danish Design School.

Working with design, Kasper believes that the most creative and interesting solutions come out of new experiences, and he always strives to be versatile in regards to method, medium, and aesthetics.

Ken-tsai Lee
Taiwan, China

Lee was born in Taipei. After establishing his own design studio in 1996, he moved to New York for his career in 2002. His partner Chou Yao-Fong keeps the studio running in Taipei. In New York, Lee has worked in different media and cooperated with professionals in other fields, such as photography and animation, in order to explore new methods of design. He was invited to be the visiting professor for Taiwan University of Arts in 2009 and still holds this post. He has also won numerous design awards and participated in many design exhibitions worldwide, such as the D&AD Award.

Kyosuke Nishida
Canada

Kyosuke Nishida is a Montreal-based graphic designer who has worked on projects ranging from graphic design to set design and environmental displays, among other things. His interest now lies in experimental typography. His collaborators are Brian Li Sui Fong, Dominic Liu, Stefan Spec, Duc Tran and Sean Yendrys, who often work with him on broad projects.

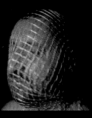

Lajos Major
Hungary

Lajos Major was born in 1973 in Hungary. She received her typography degree from MOME in Budapest, Hungary. She is currently studying for her masters degree to be a Teacher of Visual Culture at EKF in Eger, Hungary.

Lara Lozano
Spain

Lara Lozano was born in Badalona in 1989. She is a graphic designer who currently lives and works in La Bisbal d'Emporda (Catalunya), and studies at the Art and Design School of Olot. She often collaborates with the graphic designer Pau Larruà.

Linna Xu
Germany

Linna believes that good ideas come out of play and that it's worthwhile to turn off her Macbook for a day or two. Her personal design philosophy is that less is more and that wrong is probably right. She is motivated, passionate, curious, obsessive (in a good way), and drawn to the imperfect. Outside of design, Linna fiddles with photography, plays the piccolo, dances ballet, and occasionally craves algebra.

Madoka Takuma
UK

Madoka Takuma graduated with First Class Honours from Central Saint Martins College of Art & Design (UK) with a BA in Graphic Design in 2008. She currently works as a freelance graphic designer and is based in London. The fields she's most passionate about are editorial and packaging design. Madoka's taste for stylized, functional, yet economical, construction has garnered her worldwide recognition.

Me Studio
The Netherlands

Me Studio is a small independent design office based in Amsterdam. The studio's business is image, identity, and inspiration for a wide range of cultural and commercial clients, locally as well as internationally. They focus on visual corporate identities, posters, and books. The designers love each day that they work in the field of design.

Nam
Japan

"Nam" is an artist group originally established by Nakazawa Takayuki (graphic designer) and Manaka Hiroshi (photographer).

Currently, over ten artists from various backgrounds are members of NAM, united in the search for possibilities within the world of visual arts based on their shared theme of "a fantasy in life."

Nello Russo
Italy

Nello Russo is an Italian Visual Designer and Art Director based in Torino, Italy and New York, USA. He obtained a Visual Arts MA (IUAV Venezia, 2008), a Graphic Design BA and Publishing Design BA (Politecnico di Torino, 2004 and 2002). He currently works as a freelance designer and he has recently started his personal art / editorial project called SO-AND-SO for the production of a series of limited edition periodical artist monographs.

Nina Jua Klein
UK

Nina Jua Klein was born in Nairobi, Kenya and grew up in Singapore and London. In 2004, she completed her Foundation studies at Wimbledon School of Art & Design and went on to earn a BA in Typo / Graphic Design at the London College of Communication in 2008. She is currently working and living in London.

Nod Young
China

Nod Young has carved a niche in the realm of enterprises looking to make their mark both within and beyond China. As the Co-Founder and Creative Director of Khaki Creative & Design, Nod leads a team of multicultural artists and designers that uses clean and strong visuals to fulfill diverse marketing strategies. At the same time, Nod has helped to create an environment that fosters creative ideas both for himself and his team. Based in Beijing, Nod is a prolific artist whose passion lies in typography and graphic design. He draws his inspiration from myriad sources, although he is most fond of designs originating from the UK and Japan.

onlab
Germany & Switzerland

onlab, a Swiss graphic design agency, was founded in 2001 and is based in Berlin, Germany. onlab works on commissioned, collaborative, as well as content-based design and consultancy projects. onlab is co-founder of etc publications, a platform for independent publishing.

"Design is a narrative that can change how people approach the world" — that's how Andrew Losowsky, writer and editor, described onlab's philosophy in his article for the Wall Street Journal. onlab stages content with the goal of conveying relevant topics and, in doing so, obtaining a change in public perception. Content is king at onlab.

Patrycja Zywert
UK

Patrycja Zywert is a graphic designer based in London. She has a passion for typography and packaging design. She grew up in Bydgoszcz, Poland and always enjoyed drawing and learning languages. In 2007, Patrycja moved to England to combine these two interests and begin her graphic design studies. She graduated from Bucks New University in September 2010 with a degree in Graphic Arts and is now looking for a satisfying job in London.

Paul Hollingworth
UK

Currently working in the UK, Paul Hollingworth is a multi-disciplinary designer whose work spans many aspects of creative design. Despite the diversity of his work, Paul has one unifying theme that runs through everything he does: passion and determination to push the limits of even the most menial graphic tasks.

Pinky Leung
Hong Kong, China

The designer, Pinky Leung, was born in Hong Kong. He finished his Higher Diploma in Visual Communication at HKU SPACE Community College in 2007. He later completed his BA (Hons) in Graphic Design at Middlesex University (London, UK) in 2009. Pinky Leung founded a Hong Kong-based creative studio called Pink Lab. The studio works in different fields of communication design, such as corporate identities, promotional campaigns, posters, editorial design, book design and font type design. The studio's work includes both commissioned projects and self-initiated projects.

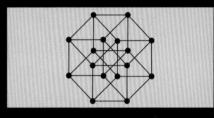

Ralph Hawkins
UK

Ralph Hawkins graduated in 2009 from the UCA in Farnham, having also studied at the University of Lincoln. He is currently working on personal projects and freelance work and is part of MoreGood.

Raúl Iglesias
Spain

Raúl Iglesias is a graphic designer from Madrid, Spain. He received his specialization in editorial design from Madrid's Istituto Europeo di Design. He currently is doing freelance work on many different projects mainly related to the arts. Raúl lives every project as a process and a unique experience. He is firmly convinced that a good concept is the cornerstone of good design.

Roger Gaillard
Switzerland

Roger Gaillard is a 24 year old designer from Switzerland. He received his BA in Visual Communication in 2010 at HEAD GENEVA. He currently lives in Rotterdam, the Netherlands, where he has an internship with DC WORKS. After that, he plans to move back to Switzerland to found his own graphic design studio. His work often focuses on the opposing relationship of science and instinct. He loves finding poetry in science, and science in poetry. He defines himself as a human robot.

Romualdo Faura
Spain

Romualdo currently works as a freelance graphic designer in Murcia (Spain) with a background in corporate branding, icon design, illustration and editorial projects. He undertook doctoral studies on the Education of Ethics in design studies at the University of Murcia, and has taught subjects such as corporate identity, editorial design, typography, presentation skills, and architectural design portfolios in various schools and universities in Mexico, Guatemala and Spain.

Sasha Prood
US

Sasha is a designer, illustrator, artist and devotee of all things paper. She specializes in typography, illustration and pattern design in the mediums of pencil, pen and watercolor. She pursues balancing her art and design, concentrating on work that is a melding of handwork and the computer. She always has a sketchbook with her in order to jot down new ideas and inspiration. These days much of her inspiration comes from science, nature, traditional cultural practices and vintage, utilitarian and childhood items. It is wonderful to be able to pursue work based directly on what inspires her in daily life.

Sergio Alves
Portugal

Sergio Alves is an emerging young designer based in the city of Porto in northern Portugal. Sergio's designs are not limited to a specific school or idea, but rather are often based on art & craft or the use of organic materials within the design process. Each project may differ greatly from the previous project, as he experiments with new mediums and allows each project to dictate the best way to communicate the theme. Today it may be a cut-up carpet, tomorrow a hand-painting or a photograph; he continually pursues creative and experimental design with a fresh approach to each new project, avoiding the expected and seeking always to surprise.

Shaz Madani
UK

Shaz Madani is a designer based in London. Originally from Tehran, Iran, she studied Graphic Design at the London College of Communication. Since graduating in 2008, she has been involved in various projects ranging from identities and branding to magazines and books.

Sixstation Workshop
Hong Kong, China

Sixstation was founded in 2008 by Benny Luk and currently operates in a SOHO (Small Office Home Office) form. Backed by experienced and award-winning expertise in the design field, Sixstation Workshop provides professional services for branding, web design and visual identity packaging with a strong design sense including illustration and typography.

Snask
Sweden

Snask creates ideas, design and communication. We tell stories of great times and create identities that will make you scream, kiss and tell. We design brands, books and lifestyles. Hello and Snask Off!

Staynice
The Netherlands

Staynice is two brothers, Rob and Barry van Dijck. Their motive is to leave something personal behind, something that lasts. Ever since they were young, they have felt drawn to this. The need for it has only become stronger. Staynice has its roots in the graffiti and street-art movements. This is directly shown in the unadjusted way the brothers work, turned into a powerful visual style. Their core business is printed matter. Hand painted wall graphics are also an important part of their portfolio.

Stefan Sagmeister
Austria

Stefan Sagmeister, a native of Austria, received his MFA from the University of Applied Arts in Vienna and, as a Fulbright Scholar, received a masters degree from Pratt Institute in New York.

He has designed visuals for the Rolling Stones, the Talking Heads and Lou Reed. Having been nominated five times for a Grammy award, he finally won one for the boxed set he designed for the Talking Heads. He has also won many international design awards.

Studio mw
France

Mw is a graphic design studio founded by Jeanne Moinon and Pierre-Olivier Thiriet in 2009 in Kremlin Bicêtre (a suburb of Paris). Their work centers on printed design for public, private and institutional partners. They also perfect their "savoir-faire" style through artistic collaborations and experimental research aiming to create a conceptual impression that echoes into personal graphic sensibilities.

Sveta Sebyakina
Russia

Sveta Sebyakina is a graphic and type designer. She's also a teacher at British Higher School of Art and Design. She currently lives in Moscow and works as an Art Director at the Republica design studio. The team works on a variety of projects, including identity, branding, and graphic design.

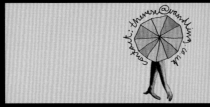

Therese Vandling
UK

Therese Vandling is a London based graphic designer, illustrator and printmaker. Having studied at the London College of Communication (BA hons) and the Royal College of Art (MA), she now works as a jacket designer for a London publishing company as well as taking on other freelance commissions.

Thinking*Room
Indonesia

Thinking*Room is a graphic design studio based in Jakarta, Indonesia.

"We design, we make things simpler, we refuse to grow up, we listen to you, we try to make culture, we support each other, we dislike arrogance, we pet our dogs, we play music when working, we do not watch television, we are having a hard time cleaning up our place, we work for charity, we hardly turn the lights on while working, we see things upside down, and we love you."

Thom Bradley
UK

Thom Bradley is a 22 year old graphic design graduate from Kingston University, London. He is passionate about communicating strong design ideas as well as executing projects with a strong, appropriate aesthetic. Typography is something he has always been interested in from an early age, and a lot of the self initiated work he has completed stems from this.

Thom Isom
UK

Thom Isom is a creative graphic designer based in Lancashire, England. Thom enjoys geometry, porridge and music strictly from Scandinavia. He specializes in branding, print, promotion and mixed media graphics but sees a fine line between all areas of art and design. He graduated from De Montfort University, Leicester in June 2010 with a first class honours degree in Graphic Design. He now does freelance work for clients based in art, music and fashion.

Tiana Vasiljev
Serbia

Born in Subotica, Serbia in 1985 and currently a London-based freelance designer, Tiana graduated from the Enmore Design Centre, Sydney in 2006 with an Advanced Diploma in Graphic Design. She began her design career in 2007 freelancing for Valentine Associates, a multi-disciplinary Sydney-based design studio. Tiana continued to work at Valentine Associates on a range of work including branding projects, logos, corporate literature, brochures, catalogues and editorial layouts until the company closed its doors in mid 2009. With a special emphasis on typography, attention to detail, a strong conceptual attitude and a willingness to experiment, she is open to all challenges.

Tim Fishlock
UK

Tim Fishlock is a designer / artist based in London. He began his creative career fabricating the designs of Thomas Heatherwick and has gone on to produce artworks and print design for clients such as Paul Smith, Electronic Arts and Habitat. Tim recently finished an eighteen month stint at The Partners so he could concentrate on his own projects.

Topos Graphics
US

Topos Graphics is a multidisciplinary design studio based in Brooklyn, NY. The studio strives to create meaningful and visually intriguing answers to print and web questions. The designers' job in part is to make clients look as smart as they actually are, creating online and printed matter that is memorable and sometimes collectible. They do this through the processes of research and investigation, employing a wide range of tools with a vast knowledge of the best resources in NYC and the world. Topos Graphics maintains direct working relationships with clients, from concept to the finished work.

TwoPoints
Spain

TwoPoints.Net was founded in 2007 with the goal of doing exceptional design work: work that is tailored to their clients needs, work that excites their clients and customers, work that hasn't been done before, and work that does more than work.

Type Fabric | Atelier für Gestaltung
Switzerland

Type Fabric consists of Catrina Wipf and Samuel Egloff from Lucerne, Switzerland. After studying Graphic Design together, the studio Type Fabric was founded in the summer of 2009. In the summer of 2010, they became part of Edition Typoundso, a self-publishing group.

Victor Kay
UK

Victor Kay is a young and ambitious graphic designer hidden away in the North of England.

Wei Cheng Chu
Taiwan, China

Wei Cheng Chu was born in Kaohsiung, Taiwan in 1983. He is currently a graphic designer of DDG in Taipei.

Wing Lau
Australia

Wing Lau is a designer from Hong Kong who currently resides in Australia. His design unit Krafted by Wing Lau has been based in Sydney since 2007. Through his conceptual work and content driven design, he aims to enhance the cultural sector of the community through his ways of thinking and his ability to create lasting works of aesthetic and conceptual integrity. He is very attached to bilingual typographic design integrating both English and Chinese characters. He has been researching this type of design for years after being inspired by his honors research thesis.

Winnie Tan
Singapore

Winnie Tan was born in Singapore in 1975. She graduated from Temasek Polytechnic (Singapore) in 1995 and Kent Institute of Art and Design (UK) in 1997 where she studied Visual Communication. After 10 years of graphic / multimedia design and teaching experience in Singapore, she moved to Prague (Czech Republic) to pursue an MA in Typeface Design at the Academy of Arts Architecture and Design Prague (VSUP). She is now living and working in Singapore.

Zaijia Huang
France

Zaijia Huang is a graphic designer originally from China but now residing in Paris, France.

Zwölf
Germany

Since Zwölf's founding in the year 2000, the studio's primary work has been in poster design, as well as in developing packaging, books and exhibitions, scenographic work in film and television and corporate consulting on design questions. They make use of a palette of simple colors, detail-rich typography, carefully chosen materials; and a constant experimental exhaustion of all of the many possibilities of a piece of paper. The studio's screen printing workshop in A0 format allows them to produce small batches of large-scale prints.

ACKNOWLEDGEMENTS

We would like to thank all of the designers involved for the kind permission to publish their works, as well as all of the photographers who have generously granted us the right to use their images. We are also very grateful to many other people whose names do not appear in the credits but who made specific contributions and provided support. Without these people, we would not have been able to share these beautiful works of design with readers around the world.